Infinity *in* Christ

Infinity *in* Christ

IVY OPPAN

WESTBOW®
PRESS
A DIVISION OF THOMAS NELSON
& ZONDERVAN

WestBow Press books may be ordered through booksellers or by contacting:

WestBow Press
A Division of Thomas Nelson & Zondervan
1663 Liberty Drive
Bloomington, IN 47403
www.westbowpress.com
1 (866) 928-1240

Because of the dynamic nature of the Internet, any web addresses or links contained in this book may have changed since publication and may no longer be valid. The views expressed in this work are solely those of the author and do not necessarily reflect the views of the publisher, and the publisher hereby disclaims any responsibility for them.

This book is a work of non-fiction. Unless otherwise noted, the author and the publisher make no explicit guarantees as to the accuracy of the information contained in this book and in some cases, names of people and places have been altered to protect their privacy.

Scripture taken from the King James Version of the Bible.

Certain stock imagery © Thinkstock.
Any people depicted in stock imagery provided by Thinkstock are models, and such images are being used for illustrative purposes only.

ISBN: 978-1-4908-7184-4 (sc)
ISBN: 978-1-4908-7185-1 (hc)
ISBN: 978-1-4908-7183-7 (e)

Library of Congress Control Number: 2015903432

Print information available on the last page.

WestBow Press rev. date: 3/30/2015

The Lord's Message of Freedom to Humanity

The Spirit of the Lord God is on me. The Almighty God has chosen me to bring good news to poor people. He has sent me to heal those with a sad heart. He has sent me to tell those who are being held and those in prison that they can go free. He has sent me to tell about the year of the Lord's favor, and the day our God will bring punishment. He has sent me to comfort all who are filled with sorrow. To those who have sorrow in Zion, I will give them a crown of beauty instead of ashes. I will give them the oil of joy instead of sorrow, and a spirit of praise instead of a spirit of no hope. Then they will be called oaks that are right with God, planted by the Lord, that his Holy Name be glorified forever and ever more."

Amen and Amen!

Contents

Preface

Nothing in the universe came into existence by itself, and this book recounts how that truth was revealed to me.

There is a creator behind the universe—the Lord of Hosts, the maker of all things. A part of him is Jesus Christ, our Lord and Savior, ruler of everything in heaven and on earth.

There are heavenly places where spirits reside in peace and tranquility. There is also Hades where destruction awaits the spirits of perdition.

After you read this book, you will be inspired by the resurrection power of the Holy Spirit to seek first things of the Spirits, the Kingdom of Jesus Christ while on planet earth; thereafter earthly and heavenly blessings will be our inheritances forevermore.

Amen and amen!

Acknowledgments

In this book I detail revelations given to me by Jesus Christ to share with humanity. I give glory to the Lord of Hosts, creator of all things in heaven and on earth, for salvation, grace, and righteousness through Jesus Christ, our Savior. Words alone cannot express my gratitude for his goodness and mercies, which endure forever.

I thank Jesus Christ for counting me worthy to see heavenly places and for enabling to relate these revelations of his mystery to humanity. I will always be grateful for his love and compassion for me and for his grace to humanity in revealing insights about heavenly places. By his grace I was able to see these revelations and to testify about them; may his holy name be glorified forevermore.

I am grateful to my husband, Anthony; my daughters, Josie, Daisy, and Andrea; my son, Anthony Jr., and my sons-in-law, Jody and DeCarlos, for their love and support through the years.

I would also like to thank my mentors, the men and women who have shared their wisdom, knowledge, and inspiration to strengthen me in the faith through our Lord Jesus Christ. I would still be wandering in the wilderness if not for their guidance. I am grateful to have knowledgeable men and women in the faith like them. God bless all of them in Jesus' name!

Amen and amen.

El-Elohim:
God, the God of All Creation

One Saturday afternoon as I drove down Clark Street on Chicago's North Side, a thought entered my head: *I wish I could get rid of all my worries, fears, and trials in the twinkle of an eye.* I did not have peace of mind. I had a wonderful family and a job that I liked, but I was empty in spirit.

As I pondered the issue, I drove down the street, hoping to find a store where I could buy clothing for my children for the Easter Sunday worship service. Engrossed in thought, I passed a clothing store a block away from Clark Street and Greenleaf Avenue. I pulled over, carefully put my car in reverse, and parked in front of the store. As I stepped out of the car, I thought, *Let me shop quickly and head home before it is too late because I have guests from church visiting my family this evening.* I did the shopping within an hour and left for home, never realizing that my life was about to change forever.

I made a right turn from Clark Street to Lunt Avenue, followed by another right turn to Ravenswood Avenue. About a quarter of a block from the intersection was a long, red-brick commercial building, and on the right-hand side of the building was a blue door with a cross on the upper part. I ignored the sign on the door and hastily drove past the building, intending to turn left on my way to Highway 41, which would take me to Beach Park, Illinois. However, I suddenly decided to turn around, go back to the red-brick building, and read the sign on the blue door. I did not second-guess myself but acted immediately; I made a U-turn back to Clark Street, a right turn a block away to Lunt Avenue, and another right onto Ravenswood Avenue.

In other words, I drove in circles back to the alley where the red-brick building was located. I drove slowly so I could read the sign on the blue door. To my amazement, I realized that I had seen the same blue door in a dream years earlier. I immediately pulled up, parked my car, and headed toward the blue door. When I got closer, I saw that the sign was for a church. I knocked on the door, and eventually a tall, slim man in a long blue robe answered. I asked if I could see the pastor; the man said the pastor was not around but would be back shortly, so I took a seat to wait for him. I was willing to wait because I wanted to ask the pastor why that blue door had appeared in my dream years before. As I waited, I tried to recall what else in the dream might be helpful to mention.

When the pastor had not shown up after four hours, I finally decided to leave for home, but I intended to return the next day, which would mean joining in Sunday worship at this church. Maybe then I could get my questions answered. Meanwhile, I still had an hour's drive to reach Beach Park. I was disappointed that I had wasted all of those hours, but I felt that a peace had come over me while I sat in the waiting room in the house of the Lord.

As I drove, I could hear the voices of the Enemy telling me that warfare awaited me at home, that my husband was upset with me because I had been gone too long. I drove as fast as I could, gathering the courage to face the consequences for failing to be home when my guests arrived for dinner.

When I finally pulled up on my driveway, I noted that my husband's car was parked in front of the garage. When I entered the house, my mother, Agnes Anyetei, was waiting patiently for me in the living room. I did not see my guests' car on the driveway; I assumed they had gone back home or had not shown up.

My husband, Anthony, was in the bedroom, my children were getting ready for bed, and everything was quiet in the house. When I greeted my mother, she responded wordlessly with a surprised look on her face. I quickly went into the bedroom, where Anthony was watching television. I greeted him, but he did not respond, a sign of his anger and frustration over the fact that I had not come back in time to host our dinner guests. My family was upset, and no one was willing to talk to me. That being the case, I did not explain why I was late. I took a shower and went to bed. It was an intense evening, but I kept my cool, for I knew that my Redeemer had already taken control. There was no argument on the issue, as the angels of the Lord calmed the storm on my behalf that evening.

My new faith discovery was the beginning of twenty long years of spiritual warfare and trials intended to make me give up on the will of the Father, but Jesus Christ, our Lord and Savior, never gave up on me. He stood by me and delivered me from all of the tribulations that I encountered.

The following morning was Easter Sunday. My children and I would normally have attended a worship service at the Assemblies of God church in Zion, Illinois, but on that morning, I decided to return to Chicago to that same church. A fire burned in my heart, and I had unanswered questions. In particular, I wondered why this church's blue door with its sign had appeared in my dream years ago.

I had to go back to try to find answers to my puzzle, but I could not leave my children at home on Easter Sunday. I had to take them with me to the church in Chicago instead of sending them to their regular Sunday school classes at the church in Zion.

At the time, my husband worked seven days a week and had already gone off to his job. My mother agreed to stay behind in case he returned before we did. She would be able to inform him of our whereabouts. I needed to find out what this church was all about. We left for Chicago, but I promised to be back in time for dinner. We arrived at about nine o'clock in the morning, and I was surprised to find out that the worship service did not start until ten and would not end until four in the afternoon. Still, I wanted to talk to someone after the service, so I would wait patiently until it was over.

During the service, no one paid attention to me as a visitor. Most members walked by me as they went to and from the sanctuary. I felt awkward and rejected, but my children kept me busy by asking questions about the church. I did not have the answers. This church's form of worship was completely different from what they had experienced in the Assemblies of God church; however, the music was good, and we enjoyed the service to its fullest until four o'clock. Though I had given my mother my word that we would return home as early as possible, we did not leave the church until the service was over—and then some.

It would be an hour before I could talk to the pastor. After a short introduction, the pastor called the congregation to surround me for prayers. Immediately, the resurrection power of the Holy Spirit descended on me and manifested itself as I spoke in tongues.

The congregation was surprised to hear other tongues spoken. Though I felt the resurrection power of the Holy Spirit in the church, no one spoke in tongues. There were prophets and prophetesses in the congregation, but no one was gifted with diverse tongues or with the power of interpreting them. I received the gift of diverse tongues through the grace of Jesus Christ. After the congregation members prayed for me, everyone wanted to know who I was and where I came from, so I explained that I was a newer worshipper and that this was my first day among them, Members then asked me questions including how I found out about the church. "Well, that is a long story," I said. I was not about to share my dream with the congregation until I got answers to my own questions.

My spirit, soul, and body were peaceful when I entered the sanctuary, but my questions had to wait. It was already late when the service ended, and my children were hungry, so we left to get back home in time for dinner.

Jehovah-Tsidkenu: the Lord, Our Righteousness

A person baptized with the resurrection power of the Holy Spirit experiences a rebirth forever. I began to notice a gradual transformation taking place in my attitudes toward everything. The things that once mattered to me most became secondary. As burdens were removed, the Lord's peace entered my life, and I slept untroubled through the night.

The Enemy was not happy about my rebirth. He had had me under his spell, running my life and bringing me torment and grief. He increased my troubles, and it seemed that when I was relieved of one, another would appear in its place. I suffered bad dreams and night terrors. However, the Lord delivered me out of all my trials. Today I can testify to the world that there is power in the blood of Jesus Christ, who redeems souls from troubles. We just have to reach out to him in faith.

The church in Chicago was a perfect one in that the supreme power of the Holy Spirit reigned and Jesus Christ manifested himself during worship services. When we pray to the Lord, angels in the sanctuary are listening around the clock and will convey those requests. If we believe that God can hear us and will answer those prayers, instantly they are answered. I am a living testimony to that truth. The many prayers I and others offered in that church were all answered by the Father through Jesus Christ.

However, due to the lengthy worship hours and distance from my house to the church, my husband expressed concern about whether I should attend or be a member of the congregation. However, I would not allow him to make me a disobedient child or to take away my newfound peace and joy in Jesus Christ. We argued almost every Sunday after I came home over how long I stayed at church, but I persevered.

Jesus Christ and Satan were battling over my life. I was a lost soul saved by grace. Though my flesh wanted to yield to my husband's point of view, the resurrection power of the Holy Spirit burned in me. I felt I had no choice but to obey the Lord's wishes and continue to worship at the same church.

I began to experience divine messages through my dreams encouraging me to direct affairs of the church. My calling became clearer. However, the length of the worship hours, the required white worship garments, and the doctrine of the church remained issues for my family for several years.

However, none of these issues mattered to me. My focus was only on the commandment of the Lord of Hosts to do his work and on manifestations of the resurrection power of the Holy Spirit in my life during those years. I worshipped among a mostly foreign group of people and did not understand their dialect, but that did not concern me. What mattered most was that I was in the will of Father, who called me to do his work by the grace of Jesus Christ.

Who Can Overshadow
the Glory of God?

Seven years earlier, the Lord had given me a dream in which I saw myself wearing a long white robe with a cross, holding a Bible in my hand, and going to church. When I awoke, I laughed about what was shown to me in the dream. I mumbled to myself, "Are you kidding me? What was that dream all about? Am I supposed to join a church with worshippers in white garments?" There was no way that I would allow such a thing to happen to me.

Though I was content with my lifestyle, had a job, and could afford every fleshly desire, I was, as the Scriptures say, poor, wretched, and miserable. I had all my worldly wants met, but Jesus Christ was missing from my life. I knew who he was and had served him diligently years before I had gotten married, but now I had backslidden into a world full of ungodliness. My life was empty without Jesus Christ; my soul was thirsty for the spirit of the Lord that once occupied my heart.

Though my early years were dedicated to serving him, when I started my family, everything changed. My busy schedule replaced the Lord's agenda in my life. I seldom read the Bible, prayed, or attended church services. My spiritual life was on hold for years, with the Bible sitting on a shelf in my living room.

I was blind and did not realize that I had gone astray from my Lord and Savior, who had called me out of darkness into his marvelous light years before. I was not aware that I had backslidden from his ways of righteousness into darkness by my lack of fellowship with him. I did not see what was wrong. Life was good as far as I was concerned. I was content in the flesh. I did not realize that I was empty in the spirit until that fateful Saturday afternoon when the revelation that the Lord had given me seven years earlier was fulfilled in that church in Chicago.

As the Lord had revealed to me in the dream, this was a white-garment church, but I had to obey him and worship there. His will must be done on earth as it is in heaven. The dream manifested itself on that Easter Sunday, and the clue was that blue door on the red-brick building. I became a member of the church, even though my questions remained unanswered. All I knew was that the Lord of Hosts had given me a revelation and fulfilled it. However, this congregation was made up mostly people from other nations. Spiritually I was fine in this church, but at times I felt left out and could not relate to the members because of language barriers. Still, I joined to obey the Lord's purpose and not my own desires. I was not looking to make friends, to socialize, or to gain the approval of others. I was there to please Jesus Christ, who had called me to be used for his glory. That was enough reason for me to persevere.

One morning my mother said to me, "My daughter, I am so happy now that you joined this church. You are happier than ever before. I will return home in peace, knowing that you will be fine in the hands of the Lord!" I smiled at her and replied, "I am happy to know that you approve of my newfound faith in Jesus Christ. Thank you for the inspiration." Later that month, my mother went into cardiac arrest and passed away at Victory Memorial Hospital in Waukegan, Illinois.

For several years, I could not get over her loss. I blamed myself, asking what I could have done differently and wishing I had another chance, but she left suddenly and was in our Lord's arms forever.

Life is far more important than earthly treasures. The things of this world can always be replaced, but lives can never be replaced. Only Jesus Christ can resurrect a soul back to life. We must spend every moment loving one another and cherish every second of our lives, knowing that life is precious and fragile and can never be regained once it is taken away. It is gone until the day of rapture when all spirits will be resurrected back to life by Jesus Christ.

Christ, the Eternal Glory

During one Sunday morning service, the resurrection power of the Holy Spirit visited the congregation mightily. It came upon me and I was slain in the spirit. The power came as a rushing wind and was so strong that I could not resist its force. I fell down on the church floor and yielded to the will of the Holy Spirit to sanctify me for his use. I felt the anointing oil penetrating my whole body. I could not open up my eyes or move my muscles, but I could hear music. The more intense the worship music was with praise, the more anointing fell on me. After a while, the oil became painful, like nails penetrating my body. The pain was more excruciating than childbirth. I felt like thorns were piercing me from head to toe. I am not quite sure how long the pain lingered, but it seemed like a long time.

Those painful nails seemed to crucify me to the carpet on the floor of the sanctuary. I could not open my mouth to say how I felt or to report what was going on with my body. Since I could not move my muscles, I wasn't able to get up from the floor. The excruciating pain continued to distress my soul. I could not open my eyes. Time ceased to operate. Everything was in a now mode. I was not conscious of my environment, the people around me, or the time of day. I was solely in the spirit, with my soul listening to the music.

Suddenly, the music started to fade away and my inner eyes were opened. Though I was inside the sanctuary, the roof no longer restricted my view and I could see the skies above me. They grew clearer and brighter as the clouds vanished. I did not observe my spirit leaving my body, but I was somewhere in the atmosphere trapped among demonic entities trying to break through their world into the firmament of glory. I presumed that prayers were being said for me in the church, but I knew that I was in another realm altogether. I no longer felt the pain and could not remember what had happened to me physically. I was somewhere among the forces of darkness.

Between heavenly places and earth is a world made up entirely of principalities and the powers of darkness. To reach my destination, my flesh had to be crucified. This would provide me with spiritual armor, empowerment from the Holy Spirit through Jesus Christ to proceed on the journey.

The task was not easy. I met principalities of all sorts in the demonic realm. There is indeed a demonic kingdom operating between heaven and earth. It is not a joke, and though we do not see these entities, they are with us at all times. They plan evil for the children of the Lord, lead them to it, and mock them for their failures. These ugly beings are crafty and full of evil. I asked myself, *Why am I among these entities, and how did I get here?* But there was no time to second-guess myself. They hindered me from moving to the next level of my journey to the firmament of glory.

Throughout this experience, the church kept a prayer vigil on my behalf. After a while, I assumed that the worship service had ended and that some members had left for home. Therefore I had less spiritual support to press on through the kingdom of darkness to my destination. I was trapped between earth and heaven in the demonic world.

I was ridiculed and tormented by demons, who said, "You cannot go anywhere. You are a sinner. You are already condemned, and nothing can save you." They laughed and called me all kinds of names, saying, "You are full of iniquities. You are not pure or worthy. Where do you think you are going? You belong to Hades." As they ridiculed me, the demons formed a barricade, blocking me from getting through to the next level on my journey to heaven.

These dark entities used extended body parts to hang on to each other and block my way. I do not recall speaking to them or praying. I simply pressed on, attempting to break through their barricade with my hands while they continued to insult and mock me.

At this point, I could no longer hear earthly noises or music from heavenly places. I was completely out of touch with the world, trapped between earth and heaven. My body had been crucified by those painful nails, and there was no return to earth for me yet. I had to succeed in my journey, but I could hear nothing except for those voices insulting me and laughing. The entities continued with their evil works to discourage my spirit from getting through to the firmament of glory.

The Enemy is a crafty liar. He can change his looks to make us believe that he is a messenger of good will from the Father, only to get us to walk into his devilish traps of destruction. When he succeeds in leading us astray, he will come up with allegations and condemnations.

Let us be more careful about what voices we heed; the Enemy is crafty and full of evil works.

As I tried to break through their territory, the entities tormented me more, pushing me backward to earth with their evil barricades, but their efforts were in vain. Suddenly, a presence came over me out of nowhere in a bolt of light and scattered them. I was delivered from the bondage of Satan and set free forever.

The atmosphere immediately became brighter and clearer, and I was able to break through the demonic realm and proceed into the arms of Jesus Christ. I could not precisely identify the force that had delivered me. All I knew was that the hand of Jesus Christ had reached out to me right after the divine intervention.

Hallelujah! Jesus Christ had won the victory over the Enemy again, saving a lost soul. I was set free and released into the celestial realms. Glory be to the Father, the Son, and the Holy Ghost forevermore. I later learned that messages came to the church through prophecies that the congregation should say intensive prayers on my behalf to make sure that I was doing all right in the spirit. I was not awake or moving my muscles, but I was still breathing normally. Members of the congregation continued to pray and to sing, and that may be the reason I was not defeated in my battle with the demonic entities before our Lord's intervention.

Hallelujah!

I give all glory to the Lord, who created everything in heaven and on earth, and before humanity I reveal all that was shown to me by Jesus Christ, who gave me permission to do this.

As soon as I was able to pass through the world of darkness, the angels welcomed me with songs of hallelujah, sounding trumpets at the heavenly gates. Jesus Christ, the Lord of Hosts, stood there illuminated with glory and led me into his kingdom.

There is nowhere else like heaven! Let us all strive to get there. No words can describe this amazing and peaceful place. Enormous lights in many colors beamed at me; they were so bright that I could hardly see through them. I realized that I was in the realm of light among angels. I had been transformed from flesh into spirit. I saw through the lights the hands of our Lord, beckoning me to come. I felt the warmth in my spirit and saw love and compassion in his eyes when he spoke to me. I ran toward Jesus, and he received me in his arms with a smile. His eyes beamed as intensely as the lights, and his garments glowed like the sun and moonlight put together. The palms of his hands still bore the marks from the nails of his crucifixion. His voice thundered throughout the firmament when he spoke to me. No sound on earth could equal the depth of his voice.

The lights were so bright that there was no trace of darkness anywhere. The scenery was more beautiful than anything on earth. I could not see the beginning or the end of this enormous space. A melodious music echoed everywhere in the firmament of God's glory.

Peace and joy entered my spirit as Jesus said, "Come with me and I will show you where the Father dwells. I will tell you everything that you need to know about my kingdom in heaven."

Heaven's Golden Streets

I discovered that the streets of heaven are made of pure gold and shine like crystals. Brilliant rays of light formed rainbow colors everywhere. Words can never fully describe the glory of heaven. We must all seek the grace to someday reach heaven and see it for ourselves.

Jesus took me on a tour of his kingdom. Buildings were higher and mightier than the tallest structures on earth. Beautiful flowers bloomed with no signs of fading or withering. Music poured from the gardens as the flowers sang songs of praise to the Father of all creation. I was amazed by the flowers and the fields of green grass beside the pavement. The grass was greener and softer than any we see on earth. At more than one point during our walk down the streets, I was distracted by the beauty of the environment. There is nothing like it on earth and humanity will never do better that what has come from the Father.

I saw crystal-clear rivers flowing peacefully through the fields of flowers. Up close, the waters looked like liquid diamonds, but from a distance they resembled liquid mercury. The rivers ran gracefully without beginning or end. What an amazing God! I tried to get a glimpse of everything around me. My spirit was nourished simply by looking at the streams of living water, which Jesus had spoken of while he was on earth.

Heaven's gates are made of pearls with gold trim. They were much higher and larger than any gate on earth. The gates were so mighty that I could see structures only from a distance. However, when we got closer, the gates opened by themselves to allow us into heavenly inner courts and the Holy of Holies, where we enter the presence of the Lord of Hosts. Heaven and earth belong to Jesus Christ. He runs the affairs of both dominions, and the universe is under his authority.

The Father placed all things under his authority as a reward for sacrificing himself. Jesus took away all our sins by his sufferings, his death on the cross, and his resurrection from the dead. He triumph our death and the Adversary. The Father made him King of Kings and Lord of Lords, and he reigns forevermore.

As we proceeded along the streets of pure gold to the Holy of Holies, Jesus placed his hands around my shoulders. I felt strengthened by the intensity of his love and compassion and by his mercy and kindness toward me. Jesus spoke in a deep voice that shook the streets, but his words were full of comfort and assurance, so I was not afraid or overwhelmed by this divine encounter. In fact, I felt more confident and at home than I did on earth. Jesus and I passed through the golden gates one after another. As we approached them, they opened by themselves. My human mind could not comprehend what I was permitted to see as we walked along the golden streets of heaven. Jesus told me not to be afraid but to have confidence in him and said, "Someday this is where you will reside with me forever."

Finally, we arrived at the Holy of Holies, entering the presence of the Lord of Hosts, creator and owner of all things. The light was so bright that no human eye could penetrate it. The Father dwells in light. He himself is light, and this light is brighter than any human can comprehend, brighter than all the lights in the firmament of his glory. The light was so intense that I could not make out his face.

However, the Father welcomed me in a voice even deeper than His Son's. When he spoke heaven shook with his thundering voice and the power of his words. Fear entered my spirit, as if I were facing the most terrible thunder and lightning. I immediately prostrated myself in his presence.

The Lord of Hosts said, "My daughter Ivy, welcome to my holiness. How are things on earth?" I felt so humbled in spirit that I kept my face down and remained prostrate before him as he spoke. He did not ask me to do this, but I knew what was required of me on my first visit, so I reverenced him. "There is a reason you are here in my presence today," he said. However, the major reason I was pulled from the earth to be in his presence was placed in my spirit to be revealed only at the appointed time. I could remember only what he allowed me to share with humanity.

We are all God's children and he loves us all. Many will say that it is written in the Scriptures that no one can see the face of the Lord and live. That is true, but what it means is that no flesh can see the face of God and live. However, Moses spoke with the Lord of Hosts face to face by his grace and lived. Also note that I did not see the Lord in my physical body. My flesh was crucified on earth so I would be transformed into my spiritual body and gain access to the spiritual realms.

I have been given access to the throne of grace on several occasions. I appear before the Father mainly to pay homage to him and to receive instructions about my responsibilities in the spirit and in earthly affairs. When I appear in heavenly places, I am usually performing assigned duties or receiving wisdom and knowledge from Jesus Christ. I visit the throne of grace to reverence the Father of all creation, and on earth, I will always bow my head before him in prayer.

Regardless of how proven we are as God's children, we must realize that sin cannot come near him. Though Jesus Christ forgave us of all our transgressions, if we continue to walk in sin and our hearts are not pure and we fail to love one another, when we die, we cannot see the Father or enter into his holiness. I also want to be sure that humanity hears this testimony correctly. I was not more righteous than anybody else on earth. I did not pray for grace to enter into God's presence, nor did I gain access by my own efforts. It was given to me by the grace of the Father through the righteousness of Jesus Christ.

In the firmament of God's glory was music so melodious that no instrument on earth could bring forth such sounds. I felt peaceful and happy in his presence. There was nothing fearful about his throne, at least the part revealed to me. The love and compassion in the Father's words strengthened me. I was not afraid in his presence but was happy to be there and to be counted worthy to be given access to the throne of grace. I give glory to the Lord of Hosts, creator of all things in heaven and on earth.

When Jesus introduced us, the Father spoke to me from the throne of lights. Around the throne were angels standing like statues and wearing steel garments with swords at their sides. Some angels had large wings on their shoulders and smaller sets below. Angels floated around the throne. I could not see their feet because there were covered with luxurious garments. There were also miniature angels around the throne, and as the music echoed throughout the firmament their wings opened up and closed in time. I was not given the grace to see where the music was coming from or who was producing these sounds. There was so much going on around the throne that I was not able to see everything. However, I saw indescribable creatures that could turn their faces around without moving their bodies. Though they are fearful-looking, they did nothing to frighten me.

Peace and quiet were the rule in the presence of the Lord of Hosts. Nothing moved until ordered to do so, and there was no noise besides the melodious music echoing around the throne. I did not speak to any of the saintly beings sitting around a huge golden table arrayed in golden garments with golden crowns on their heads. I did not hear them talking to each other. Perhaps they communicated in a secret language. There was no way that a living soul could see so much and relate everything to humanity without God's grace. We can reveal only those things that Jesus Christ allows to come out of our spirits. I believe that some secrets were not revealed to me. Others given through this revelation remain concealed in the spirit until appointed times known only to the Father.

When the Lord spoke to me, I bowed down all the way to the floor. When I spoke back to him, my face was still on the floor as I paid obeisance to him who lives forevermore. He counted me worthy by his grace through the righteousness of Jesus Christ to gain access to the throne of mercy. This happened after the sanctification I received when my body was crucified on the sanctuary floor through the resurrection power of the Holy Spirit. The nails that crucified my flesh transformed my physical body into my spiritual body. I saw the Lord in my spiritual body while my physical body lay motionless on earth.

After the Father had welcomed me, Jesus took my hand and said, "Come with me and we will continue the tour of my kingdom. First of all, I want to take you to where my mother Mary resides with the nuns. She is in charge of them, and their duties are to make beautiful garments, robes, and regalia worn by the heavenly hosts. The nuns make all the yarns in beautiful colors and design all the robes." As soon as he said this, we left the presence of the Lord of Hosts and entered a corridor that seemed to be next to the Holy of Holies. Jesus took me to the nuns' residence and introduced me to his mother Mary. She looked young, radiant, beautiful, and full of grace. She welcomed me with a warm smile, and I bowed to her as a sign of respect.

Two points occurred to me on this visit. First, Jesus introduced his mother to me as "my mother Mary." This tells me that when we die and go to heaven, we will have the opportunity to see our saved loved ones who are already sleeping in the Lord.

Jesus also said that the nuns were in charge of designing and making heavenly robes. This tells me that when we die and go to heaven, we will not rest at all times as we have been led to believe. Duties will await us as we continue to labor for our Lord. At least we do not have to worry about paying bills; our debts have already been paid by his suffering, death, and resurrection.

After we had chatted with Mary, Jesus said there were several nuns working under her authority in the flower garden. We walked to the entrance and looked into the garden. It was beautiful. I had never seen anything greener than this grass and the leaves of these trees. The flowers were arranged in orderly rows, and their many colors formed a glorious rainbow. I was close enough to see exactly what the nuns were doing, but they were working and Jesus and I spoke only with one of their leaders. We soon left to see other areas of the kingdom. On our way out, we entered a huge hall where saints dwelled. They sat in rows around a golden table and were dressed in royal regalia, but we did not talk with them.

I saw angels busy running errands and involved in other activities. They did not stop to talk with Jesus and me or pay any attention to us. These angels did not have wings, but I was made to understand that they were messengers of the Lord of Hosts. Though I categorize all holy beings that I saw as angels, there are different types. These groupings were not explained to me, but I was made aware that not all angels have wings or dwell in the presence of the Lord of Hosts all day and all night. They have different assignments, but all work for the glory of the Father through Jesus Christ.

I saw angelic beings building mansions. Jesus showed me some of the completed rooms. Each came in different colors. The rooms had no furniture, perhaps because they were not yet occupied. Spirits rested on cottony clouds. I saw lights and colors that no one on earth can imitate except given inspiration by the Lord to bring them from the spiritual realm into the physical world.

"What color would you like your room to be painted?" Jesus asked me. I quickly replied, "I would like a sweet medium-baby-pink color. He smiled and said, "All right! That is the color we will paint your room when you come to live with us. As I already told humanity, in my Father's house there are many mansions. Now you see that everything I told humanity is true. You must go back to earth and confirm my promise about these mansions."

Hallelujah! Jesus counted me worthy to inherit the eternal kingdom with him. What an amazing grace! Praise the Lord, O my soul, and all that is within me, praise his holy name. Amen.

We proceeded to a beautiful fruit and vegetable garden. I saw fruits resembling those on earth and fruits I had never seen before. Earth is almost a mirror image of heaven, except that heaven is in the spiritual realm and everything in it resides in the spirit. Jesus came to earth to introduce the kingdom of heaven to humanity.

We produce inventions on earth with the wisdom and inspiration given us by the Father of all creation. These things are not our own inventions but come through Jesus Christ, who wants to enlighten us so that we can enjoy the earth. How could heaven duplicate what is on earth? I believe it is the other way around; every good idea comes from heaven, including the designs and technologies for road and building construction.

We visited heavenly areas further from the Holy of Holies. Here spirits in human-looking bodies lived in huge mansions. They were the Lord's messengers. Jesus explained all things to me regarding their existence and responsibilities. Many things told to me are sealed in the spirit until appointed times when heaven will allow them to be revealed to humanity. I saw administrative personnel minding heavenly affairs. I saw saints with golden crowns on their heads overseeing matters in heaven and on earth. When souls in heaven are called to serve the Lord on earth, they meet to discuss those callings. They also make decisions about souls on earth.

The spirits in heaven are aware of every storm, hurricane, and tornado that strikes earth. They see everything that will happen on earth before it occurs. They see the four corners of the world like we see the four corners of a movie screen. Though the Father created all things, he is not selfish with his supremacy; he incorporates all his saints in decision-making for the universe. Heaven knows everything that happens in our lives whether good or bad. The Enemy always seeks permission from the Father to test our faith in his righteousness before trials come to us.

These trials are different from what we allow demons to do to us because of our disobedience to the Father. There is no lawlessness in heaven; life is orderly and much more peaceful than down here on earth. When spirits make it to heaven, they are divided into working groups according to the Savior's prerogatives. In heaven, there is no day or night; spirits always dwell in light. I did not see any darkness. There are no clocks on the walls, so nobody watches the time. Maybe the spirits operate on a different kind of timing. That was not shown to me. They get things done as instructed by Jesus Christ. From my observation, they take time off to rest. Otherwise they would not have resting places, but they do not rest all the time as we are led to believe.

Jesus explained to me that all spirits in heaven have duties to perform for the Father and so cannot continually rest. That explains why they are able to watch over our souls at all times and are readily available to come to our rescue when we are in trouble.

From our point of view, it seems like heaven is far from earth, but from heaven's perspective, earth is closer than we would believe. Those in heaven can hear all of our utterances and see all of our movements because we dwell in their presence. They can hear our prayers, and every prayer comes to heaven like lightning shooting up from the earth. I saw the earth from heaven's perspective. It was darker than it appears to us. I also saw lightning coming forth from all areas of the earth. Jesus explained that these bolts were the prayers of believers sent forth to the Lord of Hosts. He said all prayers and supplications are received by angels, recorded against our names in the Book of Life, and answered by the Father at appropriate times.

Some urgent prayers are answered immediately according to our faith in him. When it comes to our utterances, we believers need to watch our mouths, for there are angels recording our spoken words at all times.

Jesus said, "I tell you my daughter, humanity will have to answer to me on Judgment Day for every useless word they speak on planet earth."

From my observation, not all spirits go to heaven and not every believer who goes to heaven becomes a saint. There is a hierarchy in heaven; spirits end up in levels of authority chosen for them by Jesus Christ. He did not explain to me how he makes those decisions, but all spirits do not reside in the same positions or abodes in heaven.

Children of the Living God

On our tour, Jesus took me to a huge orphanage housing babies from infants through four-year-olds. I saw them all arranged in rows, some in high chairs, some in cribs or nursery containers. I had never seen so many babies in one place, but on this tour, I saw them all. I was made aware that some of these babies were aborted by sinful mothers. Others had died because of medical errors, had been killed in traffic accidents or natural disasters, or had lost their lives in persecutions and massacres. They were all at the heavenly orphanage. I questioned the angels to make sure that I fully understood why these babies were there. At the end of my inquiry, I felt sad and the spirit of compassion entered mightily into my heart. I was commissioned to open an orphanage when I returned to earth.

Heavenly Places

Heaven has different levels. The Most High God and the supreme angels dwell in the holiest parts of heaven. Saints live next to the holy throne. However, there are other parts of heaven that seem to be connected to each other but are different from what was shown to me in the Holy of Holies. These areas are home to servants of the Lord who are counted worthy to inherit eternal life. I did not question Jesus about these spirits but listened carefully to him while he explained to me that they all have duties to perform for the glory of the Father. Some worshipped the Father in the Holy of Holies.

I was not made aware of any particular congregational worship; heaven is a single congregation of the living God. The angels worship the Lord of Hosts with a hallelujah chorus around the clock. Neither did I hear anyone preach the gospel in heaven. All the preaching is done here on earth, and if we refuse to listen and to be converted here, it is too late to hear sermons when we die. We either go to Hades or to heaven, and we can no longer make a choice. Humanity must hear the word of the Lord of Hosts through his servants before it is too late.

Spiritual Warfare

Back on earth, the Devil was waging a war to bring me back from my spiritual journey. From what I was told after I returned to earth, there was a different kind of warfare going on between my household and the congregation of God. My body lay motionless in the church. I was still in the spirit and had not moved a muscle in days. I was not aware of anything going on with me on earth. I could not remember that I used to exist there. Jesus and I never talked about where I had come from or how long I was to be with him in heaven. I felt so happy and excited to be with him in the spirit that I did not think I would have to return to my body.

Drama in Session

Family members and friends gathered for a meeting when they heard about what had happened to me at church. Because they were naïve about the phenomenon, friends advised my family to ask the State Department to intervene and win my release from the church. They said I was in bondage. From what I was told after I came out of the spirit, a complaint was filed against the church for holding me against my will.

The mayor's office called the church and requested my release within twenty-four hours or else the police would intervene. But how could the police release someone from the spirit? I was still with Jesus Christ in heaven after three days.

Jesus knew what was going on with my family members, the church, and the mayor's office. The church decided to pray to bring me back to earth. Jesus was aware of the church's intercession on my behalf and decided to end the tour of heaven. When he took me back to his quarters, I saw a huge golden table with a golden tablecloth. Everything on the table—cups, vases, plates, and cutlery—was made of pure gold. There were twelve golden chairs and eleven gorgeously dressed individuals. Jesus introduced me to his eleven disciples. I can still see their faces in my spirit. After they welcomed me into their midst, everyone was arranged around the table. Jesus asked me to sit in the empty chair. He said the chair was supposed to be for Judas Iscariot, but he did not make it to heaven due to sin. Jesus spoke to everyone about my assignment and ministered to us all through his righteousness.

At the dinner table, Jesus ministered the Last Supper, or Passover dinner. He took a bowl of water and a towel and washed everyone's feet, including mine. Then he wiped them with the towel while praying for us. After he had done this, we sat down in the golden chairs. Jesus said, "This is going to be your chair when you join me here again in the future." Then he took bread, broke it, and gave to everyone at the table to eat. He proclaimed that it was his body, which was crucified for all humanity, and that we should partake and live in him forevermore.

After that Jesus took a cup of wine and blessed it, saying, "This is my blood, which was shed on the cross of Calvary, given freely to drink from the cup of life. Drink and have life and thirst no more." We all partook of the wine from the golden cup. After Holy Communion, he ministered to me regarding my assignment and asked if I had any questions about his kingdom in heaven and on earth. We had a long discussion about every question I posed. Then he asked me to sit with him on the golden floor, facing each other. Before us was the biggest Bible I had ever seen, as huge as a dining table. We went through the Scriptures together. Then Jesus asked me again if there was anything else I wanted to know about his kingdom. I asked a lot of questions that cannot be recorded in this book; the Bible on earth does not include everything that happened during our Lord's ministry.

"Lord, why am I here?" I asked. Jesus smiled and said, "Because you were chosen." I did not understand why I was chosen, but he said, "You will understand later." After we searched the Scriptures some more, Jesus ministered to me and I asked a few more questions, which he answered.

Then Jesus said, "Let us go and bow down to the Father. It is time for you to return to earth. They are waiting for you."

"I like it here," I replied. "Why should I go back now?"

"Because I want you to go and tell all nations about what you have seen in the kingdom of heaven and to remind all Christian believers how important it is to partake of Holy Communion if they want to receive eternal life with me."

Jesus said that he is the only way to eternal life and that no one comes into the presence of the Father in any other way. "Anyone who does not partake of my body and drink of my blood does not belong to me and cannot be part of me in my heavenly kingdom," he said. He gave me a warm hug, overwhelming my spirit with his love and compassion. We walked back to the Holy of Holies where I said good-bye to the Father. I reverenced him once again by prostrating myself.

As I arose in my spirit from his presence, I immediately started to gain consciousness in my body inside the sanctuary. I was able to move for the first time in three days. However, I was not aware of how long I had been in the spirit with Jesus in heaven, because there was no keeping of time there.

Time is infinite in heaven. Therefore, although I did not relax or sleep, I did not feel exhausted. I saw resting places in heaven, but I was not aware of spirits sleeping and did not see them do it. I never thought to ask Jesus if spirits sleep. I did not see beds or wooden furniture, and I did not observe what spirits do in the heavenly mansions. In any event, it was always day time when I was with Jesus, and sleep would have been unlikely then.

When my spirit returned to my body and I was able to move, I saw seven church members surrounding me and praying for my return to earth. When I opened my eyes, I saw my family members in the church corridors, waiting to take me home.

Before I left heaven, Jesus promised to come back for me because there were more areas that he wanted me to see. Thank you, Jesus Christ, my Lord and Savior, for your grace. May your holy name be blessed forevermore.

When I opened my eyes, I saw my husband and a few members of my extended family. I was not too happy to see them after hearing what had happened while I was with Jesus in heaven. I could not talk to anyone when I woke up. My mouth was sore from not speaking, eating, or drinking for three days. My muscles started responding to my body movements but remained tight and sore. I felt so weak and frail that I needed help to rise up from the floor. I discovered that I had been in the spirit from Sunday morning to midnight Wednesday, a little more than three days.

Finally, my family and I left for home. At that time I could not talk to anyone about what was revealed to me. I wanted to lie down again because I was weak. When we got home, I drank water, ate some cereal, and went to sleep. My body was on earth, but I was still in the spirit. I could not explain anything to anyone yet. My husband had a lot of questions for me because he was confused about things of the spirit, but I could not answer him.

As soon as we arrived home, alas, my monthly cycle began. I was not able to return for services until it was over. In this church, when women receive their monthly cycle, they are prohibited from joining the congregation until after eight days. Then they will be clean again and can fellowship with others, according to the Law of Moses in the Old Testament. That is part of the doctrine of the church. I had no problem with this doctrine. This church was where the Lord wanted me to be. I felt spiritually charged and experienced the power of the Holy Spirit during my stay at home.

I was soon able to go back to worship, and when the service started, the first worship song sung by the choir electrified me with the resurrection power of the Holy Spirit. I was knocked back down, slain in the spirit again. The second time around, I did not feel the pains that I felt before nor was I hindered by demonic entities. The angels immediately received me at the end of the tunnel in front of heaven's golden gates and led me to the arms of Jesus Christ.

Ever Faithful, Ever Sure!

Jesus received me again, and I heard songs of praise accompanied by trumpets and other instruments. I felt happy and love filled my spirit. I felt welcomed and at home in the arms of our Lord. As soon as he received me, he dismissed the angels who ushered me into his presence, and we walked down the streets of pure gold with crystal-clear rivers flowing alongside of them.

Jesus placed his arm around my shoulders and assured me of his love and the Father's love for me and for all humanity. "I have more to tell you and to show you," he said. We were immediately in the presence of the Lord of all creation. Angels worshipped the Father, bowing down and raising their wings to pay him homage while melodious music echoed throughout the Holy of Holies.

Standing before the Lord of Hosts, I felt peace and everlasting joy. The music had a beauty unknown to humanity. I felt small in the Father's presence because there was no end to the magnitude of his throne or to the place where he dwells. I immediately prostrated myself before him when he welcomed me. His voice was deep and thundering, and his words rumbled throughout the firmament of his glory. My face was all the way down on the golden floor.

The cherubim and the seraphim fluttered around the throne. Giant guardian angels stood at attention. Angels with faces no one in the flesh can describe looked as if they were ready to attack anyone who was not authorized to be in the Father's presence. These angels could turn their faces around without moving their bodies.

It is a fearful thing to fall into the hands of the almighty God, creator of all things. He did not say much after welcoming me into his presence. However, I felt glad for the grace that Jesus Christ had given me to appear before the Father and to relate all these revelations to humanity. May his holy name be glorified forever and evermore.

O God of Mercy, Truth and Grace; I thank you and give you all Glory, Praises and Adorations; I will forever be grateful for your tender loving kindness bestowed upon me all these years; without your help in ages past; present, and future; I would have already gone down to the grave to sleep in death; what did I do to deserve your tender loving cares and your kindness towards me? When I think of all these favors; I just want to shout Hallelujah, sing songs of praises and glorify your Holy Name every day for the rest of my life. Thank you for everything!

Jesus Christ is in charge of the universe. All things are placed under him by the Father. After I paid obeisance to the Father, Jesus took me to the rest of the areas where spirits reside. In some areas, Jesus only pointed out and explained things to me from a distance, and we did not meet any of the spirits there.

Visit to Hades

Jesus showed me two doors at the judgment seat. The right-hand door led to eternal life, while the left-hand door led to Hades and damnation. The doors looked alike, but the destinations were far different. Jesus told me, "We will go to the other side so I can show you what you need to see and tell humanity. Let me warn you, Ivy, that when we go through these doors, things will change. You will see the opposite of what you saw out here, but there is nothing to fear because I will not leave you alone or forsake you. We are going in together."

I smiled since I was not sure what he was trying to say or where we were going. Jesus asked me to follow him to the door on the left. When the door opened, I thought that we were being sent like garbage bags down a shoot. On our way down into the pit, I could not see anything because the darkness was too deep and everything happened too fast. I do not recall observing anything during our descent.

We arrived at the bottom of the pit to find an unimaginably horrible scene. The smell in Hades was awful. Nothing on earth compared with it. I was frightened because everything was dark. The only light I saw came from fires, some in the form of flowing rivers, others engulfing the bodies of spirits. "Do not be afraid," Jesus told me. "The fire will not burn you. It is burning but you will not feel it. Just pay close attention to what am about to show you down here, because I want you to relate to humanity all that you observe." The spirits in Hades wailed and burned, but their bodies were not consumed or the fires ever quenched.

It was a horrific scene, but Jesus said to me, "There are wings of Hades that I will not show you because of their contents. Some areas are too horrific for you to see, filled with evil creatures, but do not worry. There is nothing to fear, but when you go back, warn people of what awaits them if they follow the ways of the Enemy."

The atmosphere was smoky, and there was nothing like open space in the pit, but Hades spread out and was divided into wings. On our right side were spaces like jail cells with iron bars. All the cells were jammed with spirits screaming at the tops of their voices. The place echoed with the sounds of spirits screaming in agony. Some souls were on fire and never stopped burning. I became afraid, but Jesus assured me, "Do not worry, my child. Nothing will hurt you." As we moved on, I saw a lake of fire burning from the ground, springing up and attacking condemned spirits descending into the pit.

When spirits receive judgment to go to Hades, they are engulfed by the rivers of fires as soon as they enter the pit.

I saw preachers holding Bibles and dressed in bishops' and pastors' attire. They called out to Jesus to save them from the torment of Hades, but he paid no attention to their pleas.

I saw condemned spirits sitting on benches with drinks in front of them. They were drinking alcohol excessively and were wailing as the fires burned their bodies. When they saw Jesus, they immediately called out to him for mercy. One of the spirits screamed at Jesus, "I do not want to drink anymore," but they could not stop and continued to burn in agony.

I saw other spirits dancing but still burning in unquenchable fires. There was no joy in the drinking and dancing. The spirits cried and screamed in pain. The fires burned while they continued to engage in the sinful acts that had brought them to the pit of destruction.

Jesus said to me, "They do not have the power to control themselves or their ungodly behaviors down here in Hades."

Other spirits burned and screamed while they confessed their sins in the darkness of their jail cells. As soon as they saw Jesus, they screamed at him for forgiveness and mercy, but he paid no attention. "It is too late for them," he told me. "They heard the preachers on earth but did not repent from their ungodly ways."

In other wings of Hades were horrific creatures. Some appeared to have wings, but these wings were more like knives or swords. I did not see them cutting anyone, but Jesus explained to me that these were wings of torment that the Enemy uses to afflict condemned spirits in Hades.

These demonic creatures afflict condemned spirits or attack souls on earth. Creatures like these also appear in front of airplanes and motor vehicles to frighten or delude operators and cause them to lose control, resulting in accidents that destroy human lives.

Demonic spirits come in many forms, but they are all black in nature. They may be as small as fruit flies or gargantuan in size. All unclean animals or creeping things are easily used by demonic forces as instruments of spiritual warfare against godly souls and to afflict spirits in Hades.

I did not see demonic angels in human form in Hades. I saw only fires, tormented spirits, huge black birds, and nasty beasts in an atmosphere of darkness with a deadly smell. All these demonic creatures fled or gave way to Jesus as we journeyed through Hades. At one point, I panicked because a spirit screamed and jumped at me unannounced when he saw us coming in his direction. Jesus goes in and out of the pit as he desires but not to heal spirits of their burns or to minister to them. He goes down there to show his chosen spirits around and to tell them about what goes on in Hades so that they can warn people to walk in righteousness and to love one another. Brothers and sisters in the Lord, Hades is real!

When spirits receive judgment to go to Hades, the door will immediately open up and gravity will swallow them into the pit of destruction. The force of gravity is so strong that there is no chance of turning back. Spirits quickly end up in the lake of fire.

Lucifer and his demonic authorities determine what punishment condemned spirits will undergo. Once that is decided, spirits will suffer those punishments forever or until the appointed time when heaven will determine what becomes of Hades and its contents.

Although condemned spirits have received judgment from Jesus before entering the pit, when they get there, Lucifer and his demonic entities will afflict them with more torments. Several punishments await condemned spirits in Hades. Regardless of what punishment they receive from Satan, they will burn and scream. No one in the pit talked or laughed with anyone. The damned do not have the privilege of communicating, laughing, or embracing each other. Torments, wailing, and grief overwhelm them at all times.

There are no days or nights or time consciousness in Hades; everything dwells in darkness at all times. Fire and smoke fill the atmosphere, which is permeated by the awful smell of deadly decay. I do not think that such a smell exists on earth. Hades is the only environment designed for such a stench. The smelly gas was coming from the evil beasts and the burning bodies in the dungeon. There were no vents providing fresh air or oxygen to breathe.

These spirits were dead when they were sent to Hades, so this was what Jesus meant by the second death. They did not possess human flesh but were spirits. Therefore their spirits, not their bodies, were burning. As we continued the tour, I realized that not all spirits were under the same punishment. Some received worse penalties than others. Regardless, they all cried out in agony to Jesus to redeem their spirits, but it was too late. They already belonged to the Adversary.

"There is nothing that I can do for them now," Jesus said with tears in his eyes. "They heard the prophets, the preachers, the evangelists, and the missionaries preach to them, but they did not heed these voices. I feel sad for them, but I cannot save them now." There was sadness in his voice. He felt sorry for these souls, but they belonged to Satan and he could no longer free them.

I am amazed at how the Devil and his demons can persuade souls to sin. When these people die without receiving salvation and end up in Hades, the same demonic entities will torment, mock, and punish them for selling their souls to the Enemy. This is serious phenomenon.

Let us be careful about what we do with our lives on earth. The Enemy is very devious in his efforts to lure us into damnation. "The Enemy is not here," Jesus said. "He cannot stand my presence. I will not take you any further. This is enough for you to know for now." As we left, I saw condemned spirits who were my schoolmates. They recognized me and called out. I had not seen them when we entered. I believe these spirits know when Jesus is around, and they run to him for mercy. I could not recall the names of these people—it had been a long time since we left school—but I recognized their faces. They told me where they knew me from. It was a sad situation, but there was nothing I could do for them. I still feel sorrowful in my spirit whenever I think about them.

"There is nothing you can do to help them now," Jesus told me. I believe there may be other spirits in the pit whom I know but was not permitted to see. Maybe Jesus did not want me to see friends who had not made it to heaven. As we left Hades, sorrow, pain, and anguish overwhelmed my spirit. With tears in my eyes, I asked Jesus, "What can I do for these spirits?" He said, "When you go back to earth, warn humanity of what awaits spirits in Hades. Everyone must choose whether to dwell in heaven with me or to burn in Hades forever."

On our way back, the resurrection power of the Holy Spirit opened the gates of Hades, and we were instantly returned to heaven places. When the tour was over, Jesus commissioned me to warn humanity of the existence of Hades and to urge everyone to walk in righteousness and to love one another.

I had another chat with the Lord about my assignment on earth and about what would happen in the future and in end times. He explained several points to me but said of the future, "This is not for humanity to know until appointed times."

He commissioned me to return to the world as his disciple, to tell everyone what was shown to me, and to bring lost souls to him. Jesus asked if I had any more questions about his kingdom and about everything shown to me. I asked a few more questions, and after a long talk, he prayed for me before sending me back to earth.

The Great Commission

After we had returned to his abode, Jesus again prayed for me and empowered me to go back to the world and preach the gospel of repentance, rapture, and his second coming. My assignment was to tell people to live in peace and harmony with one another, to resist all works of the flesh, and to worship and fear the Lord with all their hearts and souls. I was to warn people to beware of the Enemy's tricks, which could lead them to damnation, and to stress that Hades is not a pleasant place but that heaven offers peace and life everlasting. Finally, I was to tell them to love one another as the Father loves us all. Jesus said, "You now have access to heaven and can come as often as you are able. You have received transformation, enabling you to return and to communicate with me about things going on in the churches and about evil taking place on earth.

"Remember to fast and to pray that you do not enter into temptation by the Enemy. If you backslide from the faith, you will not have access to heaven until you repent and receive forgiveness and sanctification from the Holy Spirit by fasting and prayer. You are now accepted in heaven and on earth as my disciple. Go ye and tell everything that I have shown you and what you have heard from me to all the earth. As time goes on, I will work with you some more to accomplish the task ahead of you, but for now, you are free to go back to earth." After bowing to the Father, I felt sad to leave heaven and return to earth, but I had no choice other than to obey my Master's voice and do as he said.

After the commission, Jesus gave me a hug, and I felt his love and his power come upon me. I was immediately ushered into the presence of the Lord of all creation. As I looked up, his light focused on me, a sign of the Almighty's approval to go ahead. I prostrated myself before him to pay obeisance and to thank him for choosing me and for giving me the grace to appear in his Holy of Holies. As I rose from the golden floor, I opened my eyes and found myself in the church. I had no idea that I had been with Jesus for seven days. I realized that I was still human and that I had a physical body waiting for me on earth.

The entire time I was with Jesus in heaven, I thought I was functioning in my physical body. I did not realize that I was in my spiritual body. When spirits enter the spiritual realms, things on earth do not matter to them anymore. I had no memories of what had happened on earth and of how I had entered heaven until I returned to my physical body. Surprisingly, Jesus did not talk to me about the affairs of earth, but he was anxious to show and to tell me things about heaven.

Let us be aware that there is another life after death. When we die, we will live in heaven or will end up in Hades with Satan and demonic spirits. There is nothing between these two places, though others may talk about purgatory or places where spirits await reincarnation.

There are spirits in heaven who are not yet qualified to come near the Holy of Holies, but they are not condemned to Hades. Jesus gave me the opportunity to see where they reside, but I was not made aware that they were waiting to be sent back to earth.

Sometimes we tell ourselves that if we can live a righteous life on earth, we will go to heaven and rest in the arms of the Lord. I experienced a warm feeling of peace and love when I passed into the hands of Jesus Christ. However, after judgment we do not rest, as many of us believe. Jesus qualifies us to function in many areas of heaven. Every spirit who goes to heaven will be assigned to a group of angels to work for the progress and smooth running of our Lord's kingdom.

The kingdom of Christ is orderly, and everything is done according to his will. There is no disobedience to authority. Whatever Jesus says goes, and when he gives instructions no one challenges him.

Administrative personnel oversee various departments. Spirits provide services and run errands at all times. Most services are intended to help heavenly establishments run smoothly and to monitor affairs on earth.

Let us be careful. Angels are on duty at all times to listen to our conversations, prayers, supplications, and songs of praise and to report our daily activities to heaven. Everything, whether good or bad, is being entered into our records in heaven.

We must rest our bodies at the end of the day. However, angels are assigned to watch over our souls around the clock. They are either on earth by our sides though unseen or are watching over us from heaven. They are not allowed to reveal themselves to us, but they can appear in human form at any given time to save us in emergencies.

I have seen indescribable beings with wings and great illuminating lights around the divine throne.

There are angels without wings but with great lights inside their bodies and shining straight from their eyes. We cannot see them with our naked eyes but only when they choose to reveal themselves to us in the spirit on behalf of the Father.

Lastly, I believe angels take turns resting in heaven, but Jesus and I did not discuss in detail what they do. There is so much going on in heaven that everything cannot be revealed and recorded in one or two visits. That is the reason Jesus continues to reveal more of heaven to believers.

Angelic Responsibilities

1. Angels bring our spirits before the judgment throne when we pass away from the earth. Angels are on duty around the clock, recording our words and our deeds, whether good or bad.
2. Angels attend worship services with us to heal, to grant victory, and to protect and to bless us. When services are over, they report all affairs back to Jesus Christ.
3. Angels are assigned to sanctuaries all over the world and are on duty at all times to listen to prayers and to heal and to bless believers who walk in to offer them. Other angels in attendance in sanctuaries take up prayers instantly to the mercy seat for the Lord's immediate attention.
4. Angels are charged to attend to prayers wherever the Father, the Son, or the Holy Spirit is acknowledged. Regardless of time or place, they will attend to all prayers as soon as gatherings are formed by believers in the name of our Lord.
5. Angels attend church meetings held by ministers and deacons for the glory of God's holy name. They listen and offer feedback to Jesus.
6. Angels run errands, bringing messages to earth from the Father and from Jesus. There are anointing angels, ministering angels, healing angels, cupid angels, cherubim and seraphim angels,

guardian angels, administrative angels, judgment seat angels, angelic choir, warrior, and usher angels, and angels manifesting the glory of the Lord.

7. Angels are on duty to guard men and women of God who walk in the will of the Father through Jesus Christ.

The Spacious Firmament

I was made to look down to earth from heaven's perspective and was amazed that I could not see human habitations, houses, or cars. I could see only open space with objects floating in the atmosphere. Jesus views the earth through spiritual eyes. He does not move a finger or push a button to zero in on earth. The universe is always before him. He sees everywhere, knows everyone by name, and hears all conversations and prayers. No prayers are wasted before the Lord of Hosts.

Before Jesus Christ came to earth to walk among us, the Father dealt directly with his creation and ran the universe by himself. He is still in control, but he has given Jesus authority over all his creation both in heaven and on earth. When Jesus calls people to service on earth, he commissions them and grants them authority with gifts of the Holy Spirit to do his will.

Heaven's Orphanage

When the subject of abortion surfaces in the media, I try as much as possible not to get involved or to share an opinion on the issue but stay neutral and keep my thoughts to myself. I always consider the economic aspects of raising children and how negative situations can drive people to take dramatic action against unborn spirits. After what was shown to me in heaven, I do not agree with those who choose to abort the unborn. However, I do not want to be judgmental. I always pray for those who commit evil acts against these spirits due to lack of knowledge from above. These acts are not acceptable to Jesus Christ.

In the beginning the Lord of all creation commanded humanity to be fruitful and multiply and to replenish the earth and subdue it (Genesis 1:28). No matter what drives us to decide to slaughter human beings, the Lord of Hosts does not take into account economic concerns or other rationalizations. He sees our actions as transgressions.

On one of my trips to heaven, I was taken to a huge building where thousands of infants and children were being cared for by angels. This huge warehouse was like an orphanage. I was made aware that these were slaughtered infants and children. When they entered the spiritual realm their spirits stayed the same age. They would not grow any older than they were when they lost their lives. There were other children who died through sickness, persecution, and accidents, but they resided in a different section. All these spirits had been given salvation.

I was made aware that when people commit abortion out of ignorance and do not know how sinful they have been, their sins will be forgiven if they repent and pray to God through Jesus Christ. However, once they know the truth, if they choose to continue slaughtering spirits, they will face judgment. When I saw all those spirits, I did not hear any crying, but I felt sorrowful and wished humanity could be made aware of what happens to aborted babies. After the tour, I was instructed to minister to those considering slaughtering infant spirits and to speak out against committing abortions. I was also given the ministry to open an orphanage to care for deserted children. I could not dismiss this revelation from my mind. Anytime I see an infant, I recall what was shown to me. Someday humanity will realize how perverse this generation has been. Too often we preach to make people feel good about them lives, failing to reprove them for the many things they do that are unacceptable to our Lord.

The Predestined

W hen the Lord wants to do something on earth through his chosen people, he gives them their callings and assignments through their spirits. At times individuals are predestined for these things. I was born and raised in a Christian family. When I was younger, I was a sick child; my parents did not think I would make it to adulthood. My mother took me to the hospital several times, but most of these visits were unfruitful. As soon as we arrived, I would suddenly be well again before the doctors could check me out. No one could understand why. Sometimes I had a fever higher than a hundred degrees and was vomiting. If she took me to a church, I would suddenly be well. It was as if nothing had happened. My mother realized that it was a waste of time and money to take me to see doctors. Thereafter, when I was not feeling well, she would take me to a Pentecostal church.

My great-grandfather was a merchant who traded in gold, sugar, tobacco, and salt. He introduced Christianity to his community and built the first Presbyterian Church in the city of Labadie, Accra. The church is still open for worshippers and serving people today. It was an abomination for anyone in our family to attend any other church besides a Presbyterian church during those years. However, my mother sneaked out with me to midweek or evening services at

Pentecostal churches. Since I would get well whenever we attended worship services, she knew that I belonged to the house of our Lord.

The Enemy was after my life and I needed to be in the house of God at all times. My mother was made aware through spiritual revelation that I was to serve God in my adult years, but she did not tell me this until I was well over thirty years old. As I grew up, I figured things out myself. I realized that when I worshipped the Lord in the beauty of his holiness and read the Scriptures, I was always happy and healthy. I am still praying to the Lord to reveal his purpose for me. I discovered that whenever I go out of my way to follow after fleshly desires, though I may seem happy, my life will be empty and have no purpose. I will not regain that purpose until I realize that I have gone astray from faith in the righteousness of Jesus Christ and return to his arms.

The Mystery of Divinity

I had an encounter with death one afternoon. I had dropped off my children at their schools and I felt unusually tired, so I decided to take a short nap before returning to pick them up. When I lay down on the comforter, little did I realize that a dramatic event was about to alter my perspective on life. As soon as I lay down, I quickly drifted off to sleep. Suddenly I saw a copy of my body leave my body on the bed. This copy looked exactly like me and was wearing the same outfit. When my spiritual body left my physical body, I turned and looked at my body on the bed. Then my spiritual body proceeded toward the bedroom door on its way out to the world.

Unknown to me, I did not have control over what was happening to me, but before my spiritual body could go through the door, the door swung open by itself. To my surprise, Phyllis—one of my younger sisters, who does not live in the States—stood by the door. "Where are you going, my sister?" she asked. I did not reply, but she stood in my way and I was not able to pass her. "Have you thought of what will happen to your three young children?" Phyllis asked. "Who will take care of them? Please get back into your body for the sake of your three young children."

I turned around and looked again at my physical body on the bed. Then I looked at the bedroom door in front of me. My sister still blocked my spiritual body from leaving. Reluctantly, my spiritual body receded back into my physical body. Immediately, I awoke and sat up on the bed, wondering what had just happened to me. I quickly got up, walked out of the bedroom, and searched the apartment for my sister, but there was no sign of anyone having been there with me. I was the only one home.

I could not understand what had happened, so I waited for my girlfriend Esther, who was at work, to come home so I could share my experience with her. Maybe she would be able to tell me more about it. Later on that evening, when I told her of my encounter, she quickly said, "I am glad that you listened to your sister Phyllis. Otherwise you would have been dead by the time anyone found you. You had an encounter with death, but your sister stopped your spirit from departing. You had what is called a near-death experience." I was so surprised that as soon as I hung up the phone, I asked myself, *why would I die and leave my three children behind? And how did Phyllis find out that I was about to cross over to the other side to eternity?*

I am still surprised at what happened. A few years later, when I had the opportunity to relate the dream to my sister, she had no idea what had happened. Perhaps our Lord will one day explain this mystery. I did not realize that this was the beginning of many more spiritual near-death experiences.

I Glorify Jesus!

You are the Lord, let your name be glorified.....You are the Lord, let your name be glorified.....I give you glory! I give you Praise! I give you Honor! I give you adoration! I give you Thanks! You are the Lord, let your name be glorified...You are the Lord, let your name be glorified....I give you glory! I give the Praise! You are the Lord, let you name be glorified in my life forever.

Amen and Amen!

After my first near-death experience, my spiritual understanding grew. I received the spirit of discernment and I dreamed accurately about things that were manifested physically. I also dreamed about things yet to be manifested. The resurrection power of the Holy Spirit took control of my life after that experience.

Back then, I was enrolled part time in a community college while I raised three children. My life was going well in worldly terms, but I was distressed in the spirit. Things were not as they appeared. I felt empty inside. My spirit was thirsty for something, but I could not put a finger on what it was. Though I read my Bible every day, I read only through the psalms. I was not praying much and hadn't acknowledged the fact that I had gone astray from Jesus Christ. I was too busy to hear his voice calling me to come back into his arms.

The Great Awakening

One night in the same year, I dreamed that I heard melodious music coming from the atmosphere. I came out of my body again, but this time around Phyllis was not around to stop me. It was the middle of the night. Stepping out of my physical body, I followed the sound. The closer I got to the music, the more melodious it became. I heard trumpets blowing a hallelujah chorus. Angels were singing, but I could not see them. I thought that if I could get closer to the music, I would be able to see the choir or join it. I had never heard such beautiful music. It seemed to move the whole earth. As I followed the sound, it became stronger and felt closer. *I thought, I love this music and will follow it until I find out where it originates.* As I got closer, I felt happier and more peaceful.

I saw a huge tunnel. Never in my life had I seen something that big. In the tunnel I heard music and saw bright lights in different colors. Though the lights were bright, the tunnel seemed foggy. I thought, *Maybe I can enter the tunnel and see exactly where the music is coming from and why the angels were are singing.* But as I get closer to the tunnel, an energy from inside sucked me into the tunnel. I floated inside the tunnel amid the lights while the music continued. I felt the music strengthen my spirit. I saw a multitude of angels in white garments blowing trumpets. They floated in the air and seemed to be dancing. *So this is where the music was coming from*, I told myself. I became excited and eagerly approached the angels.

However, I was not able to do so because they moved deeper into the tunnel as I got closer to them. I felt like I could not control my movements much longer or what was about to happen to me. However, there was no point in turning back, because my spirit was filled with joy at the music. I had no time to think of myself, my family, or where I was going. Finally, I reached the end of the tunnel, but I could no longer see the angels who blew the trumpets. I could still hear music, but it was not as loud as it had been in the tunnel. Looking up to heaven, I saw nothing but empty space. The skies above the earth are usually baby blue with white clouds and objects such as the sun, the moon, and the stars. Here I did not see anything above, though I heard music echoing everywhere.

This place was peaceful, and an overwhelming joy entered my spirit. Nothing on earth, however beautiful or costly, can compare with what awaits us in heaven. As I left the tunnel, I was happy to arrive at my destination, but I asked myself, *what am I here for? And where am I going?* As soon as these questions entered my mind, I saw a long line of men and women from all races in different outfits— police, military, football, and nursing uniforms. Every professional uniform worn on earth was represented in the queue, and others were suits and regular outfits. I did not see anyone in white, though corpses are normally placed in white dresses and suits before burial. Almost everyone was in professional attire. I believe that we will appear this way at the throne of judgment.

I joined the queue. No one spoke to anyone else. Everyone seemed anxious to get to the table ahead. As I drew closer, I saw Jesus Christ standing behind a huge desk. On the desk was an enormous book. I had never a book that size. Angels in white robes stood on both sides of the table. Everyone reaching the table had to answer a few questions posed by our Lord as he flipped through the pages of the book. I did not hear the questions nor did I hear the conversations people had with Jesus. After these conversations, they went either to the right side of the table where angels were waiting to welcome them to heaven or to the left side where a door opened into Hades. I heard screams and wailing anytime the left door swung open for a spirit to enter.

Finally, my turn came. As soon as Jesus saw me, he asked, "Ivy, what are you doing here?" I stood before him motionless, unable to answer for a moment while I thought of how to reply. I quickly learned that I had no reason to be there. All I knew was that I had followed melodious music that took me to this point. I did know why I was there or what was going on. I joined the queue and found Jesus at the judgment table. Jesus looked straight at me while he spoke. His eyes were like beams of light that penetrated my spirit. He spoke in a deep voice that thundered throughout heaven. I said, "Jesus, I just want to bow my head." He said, "Go ahead and bow your head, but go back to earth. Your job is not completed there." I felt sad because he asked me to return. However, I had no choice but to obey. Everything is under the control of our Lord.

I bowed my head before the throne of judgment, but as I raised it I discovered that my head was on the pillow in my bed. I was so surprised that everything had happened not in my physical body but in my spiritual body. *So was that all a dream?* I asked myself. In fact, it was so real that I still cannot get the whole phenomenon out of my spirit. Anytime I hear of a death, I see the queue in heaven and my soul grieves for those spirits who will not make it to everlasting life but will end up in the pit of destruction. Eternal life in heaven and eternal damnation in Hades are both real. No matter what status we possess on earth, the queue of judgment awaits us. Everyone must face Jesus Christ. There is no other way except through him. Endless blessings await those who qualify to be joint heirs with our Lord and Savior forevermore.

The Call Continues

The same year, the Lord gave me the dream in which I saw myself in a long white robe, holding a Bible and a cross in my hand, and going to church. I had not heard of a church in the States where worshippers had to wear long white robes, but I was not going to be a member of one. My sense of status would not allow me to fellowship in a church where worshippers wore these robes. My husband would forbid me to part of such a congregation.

In the dream, I laughed at the notion. *That could never be me*, I thought. *I will not allow it to happen.* When I awoke, I was still laughing. *What was I doing wearing a white robe to church?* I asked myself, and laughed some more. I told my husband about the dream, and he joined me in the laughter, but the dream was given by the Holy Spirit and I was laughing at his resurrection power. Jesus Christ said that when he left this earth, he would ask the Father to send the Comforter, who would teach us all things. Therefore I was mocking Jesus with my reaction to this dream. I did not know better, but what he had revealed to me would come to pass, because none of his words goes unfulfilled. I did not discuss the dream again for several years, but the scene stayed in my spirit, and anytime I saw someone in a white robe, the dream surfaced and I laughed again.

After a few years, I seemed to have forgotten the dream. We moved out of an apartment building in Chicago to the northern suburbs to raise our children. In those years before the dream was fulfilled, I was unhappy in almost all areas of my life. I had a family in which love reigned, but I was miserable. I could not figure out what was wrong with me.

I decided to keep busy, so I found myself a job at a hamburger place, working four hours in the evenings after dinner. It was a bad move. I made only twenty dollars a day cleaning toilets, tables, and grills, mopping floors, and restocking salad bars. I was not allowed to take breaks, because I worked the last four hours of the day. I was so exhausted at the end of the day that I couldn't wake up the next morning to get the kids ready for school. When I received my paycheck, I discovered that I had taken home only a little over sixty dollars a week after deductions. My career at the hamburger place would not last much longer, but I could not quit right away. I had to give two weeks' notice. That meant I would have to work two more weeks cleaning up other people's messes. When the two weeks were over, I settled back again into my full-time housewife duties. What could I do to satisfy the emptiness in my soul? I could not figure things out on my own.

One Saturday afternoon, I decided to take my children for a car ride to look for a church in the neighborhood where we could attend worship services. We found one about fifteen minutes from home. It was an Assemblies of God Pentecostal church. "Yes!" I exclaimed. "I like the Assemblies of God churches. Hey, kids, we will go to church every Sunday now!" Joy and peace filled my soul. The next morning, I got the children ready and off we went to worship the Lord. I saw the happiness and excitement in their eyes. Now they could go to Sunday school, join an Awana Club, and make new friends.

At the dinner table that evening, I felt the Lord's presence, and I knew that my life would change for the better. I had found the Lord and was now in his will. My children were so excited that they could not wait to go to church on Sundays. We did not attend midweek services, only because the kids had to go to school the next morning. Finding a place to worship was the biggest breakthrough in my life. My spirit was enlightened, and I felt good about myself. Gradually, the Lord did his work in my life. I found fulfillment each week at the church service, and joy started to creep back into my life. Jesus had won the battle against the Enemy.

My mother, Agnes, was visiting the family to spend time with her grandchildren. I was glad that she had come because I needed help so I could get a break from the house and find myself a full-time job. Originally, she was to spend only three months, but I convinced her to stay on a little longer to help out with the children while I joined the work force. I signed up with a manpower agency and worked temporary assignments, but I was miserable on most of them. This was not what my soul needed. What was missing in my life was Jesus Christ.

It was during that time that I decided to go shopping for the kids' clothing and was moved by God to attend a different church several miles from home in Chicago. My family was not happy with my newfound church or its doctrine. After returning home from my first Sunday service at the new church, I sat down with my mother at the dinner table and announced my intention to start worshipping in the Chicago church.

I saw the disappointment in my children's faces. They preferred to keep worshipping in the Assemblies of God church in Zion where they could attend Sunday school, the Awana Club, and summer camps. However, they did not express any concerns but agreed to try out the new church with me. My mother had already said how happy she was that I had found this church. She saw the excitement in my eyes when I returned home from the worship service that day. She knew that my spirit was being transformed. That was the beginning of my journey with the Lord of Hosts and Jesus Christ.

I never gave up on the Lord's commandment to go and serve him, and by his grace I was able to persevere throughout all trials.

Call to Service

When the Lord of Hosts calls souls for his use, he does not forsake them, and if they are faithful to his calling, they will see a manifestation of his glory. When I stepped into the will of the Lord of Hosts in my newfound church, spiritual warfare troubled my soul almost daily. I experienced terror and torment in dreams and visions. The Enemy was at war with me. *What did I do wrong?* I asked myself, but I could never find an answer.

The Lord spoke to me in a dream one morning. I did not see his face, but I heard his voice call my name three times. The first time, I did not think I heard my name, because I was not expecting anyone to call me in my sleep. Then he called me again. This time I responded and looked up to heaven to locate the person who had called me. Then he called the third time. When I said, "Yes, Lord," he spoke from among the branches of a tree. When I looked up, a mist fell on me from where he had spoken, so I could barely see his face. "Go and do my work," he said. "Yes, I will, Lord," I replied.

I was standing at the banks of a river by the tree. He called to me from the branches of the tree, so I walked over to it and looked up to locate his face, but I could not see it because of the misty showers from the tree. The encounter was so real, but when I awoke I found myself still lying in bed. *So was that a dream?* I asked myself, but it was not a dream. The Lord of Hosts had called me into his service and my life would change forever.

One Sunday morning, my husband decided not to go to work so he could spend time with his children. I left for church without them. When the service was over, I stayed to help others with prayers and to clean up the church. To serve the Lord means to serve his people and taking care of his business. Therefore I could not leave for home immediately after the service but had to work for him in any way I could, not just in the church but anywhere on earth. My family did not appreciate my dedication to the church, but I continued to do what I was commanded by the Lord of Hosts to do. This was not easy, but the Lord continued to be faithful to me by keeping me healthy, delivering me from all Enemy attacks, protecting my family members from all dangers, and allowing me to do his will.

I became more active and happy even though the Enemy did everything possible to make me break the commandments of the Lord. He could not succeed no matter how hard he tried to stop me. He was not able to prevail, for Jesus was with me throughout my walk in faith.

Divine Visitation

After a while, the Lord appeared to me again in a dream. This time he called me thorough the sun. I heard my name three times. I looked up but could not find who had called me. I replied, "Here I am," but saw no one in the cloudless skies. I saw only the sun, shining intensely. Then the Lord said to me, "Look up into the sun. I am in here." But when I tried to look into the sun, I was not able to see who had called me. The light was too great. I replied, "Lord, I cannot see your face. The sun is too bright for my eyes." He then told me, "Go to any wilderness area and I will meet with you there." I said, "All right, Lord. I will do that!"

Then I woke up and realized that this was a dream. I immediately knelt and prayed, offering thanks to the Lord of Hosts for his manifestation. I recorded the dream and the instruction given to me. However, I could not find a desert since I lived in the city. I spent months wondering why the Lord wanted to meet with me in a desert. I did not know where to find one. I am still praying that one day I will have the opportunity to meet with him in a desert.

Today God is still calling workers to do his will just as he did with Moses, Joshua, and Gideon. Are we ready to answer the call? If we should hear his voice, let us not ignore him but obey him, for he is the Lord of all creation.

Valley of Shadow

My mother was supposed to spend three months with me but ended up staying for three years. She was the friend I never had, my confidante, and adviser. I still grieve over her death, but she is in a better place with the Lord.

It was a Labor Day, exactly three years since she had arrived. My mother wanted to go back home and spend time with my siblings, and all of her suitcases were packed. I wanted her to stay much longer. I intended to throw a party and invite a few friends over to say goodbye to her. She reluctantly agreed to my idea but was not too happy about it. She seemed generally unhappy but assured me that she was doing all right.

That evening she called me from her bedroom. I was not asleep, so I rushed to her room. I found her sitting up on the bed. I asked if she was all right, and she complained about chest and stomach pains. I gave her a glass of milk. After drinking it, she said that she was doing fine, but her blood pressure was too high, so I suggested taking her to the emergency room for a blood pressure screening. My mother hesitated but agreed to go. She dressed herself and we left for the hospital.

After the screening, I was told to wait a little longer for more testing because my mother had had a minor heart attack. A few hours later, I was informed that she would have to stay overnight for further observation. Little did I know that she would not live another twenty-four hours; I stayed by her side for another three hours. Hospital personnel did as much as possible but could not stabilize her blood pressure, so they decided to hook her up to a monitor. They told me to go home and to come back the following day when they expected my mother would be able to return with me. I went back home to bed.

The next morning when I returned to the hospital, my mother was still hooked up to the blood pressure monitoring machine. I asked about her condition and whether she could go home with me. "We have not been able to stabilize her blood pressure," her doctor said. "It keeps fluctuating, and we cannot release her in that condition. I am afraid we have to keep her again tonight." I pulled up a chair at her bedside and chatted with my mother. She seemed perfectly fine except the machine was still transmitting the warning that her heart was in trouble. Pill after pill, the hospital staff tried to lower her blood pressure, but more pills without food made her sick to the stomach. After my short visit, I promised to be back again in the morning and left.

When I arrived home, I was hungry, so I ate dinner. Right after dinner, I received a call from the hospital asking me to come back because my mother's condition had worsened. "What!" I exclaimed. I immediately dropped the phone, grabbed my car keys, and headed for the hospital. When I arrived, the door to my mother's room was closed. As I turned to go to the front desk to inquire about her, I was told to step into the waiting room. I knew something was wrong, but only the doctor could tell me. Finally, the doctor arrived.

"What happened?" I asked. "Well," the doctor replied, "she went into cardiac arrest and we could not resuscitate her. She passed away." I screamed, "Are you kidding me?" I sat down on the floor in the hospital corridor, not knowing what to do. I felt like the ground was caving in on me and I was sinking into a hole. The world seemed to be following me into the hole. I felt like I was being buried alive, but Jesus Christ took control of all my troubles and I was able to get my mother ready to return to her home for burial. I thought all my travel expenses were included in the funeral home costs.

Alas, when I arrived at the airport, the airline weighed the casket and charged me by the pound. I was not aware of this expense and had not prepared for it. To my surprise, I owed the airline $8,500. In preparing for the trip, I had already exhausted our savings, and our credit cards were all maxed out. "Well, we cannot help you, madam," said an airline crew member. "But I already paid for my ticket and was booked to go on this flight. So what do I do?" I asked. The airline called a higher official, who made a few phone calls, and I was told I could make a five-hundred-dollar down payment and pay the rest of the bill in installments. I thanked the Lord of Hosts. I could not have done anything about this situation. The problem was solved by the grace of Jesus Christ, who took control of the funeral, the burial, and the aftermath.

When I returned to the States, I received a phone call from the airline regarding the bill. I explained that I had not yet started working and had made arrangements to pay off the balance by installment. However, a month later when I called the airline to start making the payments, I was told that I owed nothing. "You do not understand," I said. "Check your records."

"Yes, you did owe some money, but you do not have an outstanding balance. The entire bill has been paid off," the airline representative said.

"Can you tell me by whom and how the bill was paid?" I asked.

"Well, think of it this way: your debt has been paid off."

I thanked the representative and hung up. I immediately called my husband, who was at work, and gave him the news. He did not believe me and said, "Let me call them and verify what you are saying. There must be a mistake." He called the airline and was given the same information. The debt had been paid in full. But who paid the bill? I still do not have a clue, but I believe that this happened through the mercy of Jesus Christ, and I will always be grateful to the vessel who was used to comfort a sorrowful heart. Thank you, Jesus!

GOD OF OPEN DOORS
(Angelic inspired Song given to me by Spiritual revelation)
Open the door of Blessings for me!
Open the doors of Mercy for me!
Open the doors of Victory for me!
Open the doors, Jehovah for me.
Open the doors of Salvation for me!
Open the doors of Grace for me!
Open the doors of Heaven for me
Open the doors, Jehovah for me.
(Ivy Oppan-2013)

This world and its contents are all vanity and vexation of the spirit. Humanity does not appreciate everyday blessings from the Lord of Hosts through the grace of Jesus Christ. We enjoy grace every minute of our lives. We need to pause, to be thankful, and to give him all the glory. No matter what our circumstances are, we should be thankful and trust Jesus Christ to take control of our lives and to grant us everlasting peace.

Jehovah-Jireh:
the Lord, Our Providence

One afternoon I was feeling broken down physically, emotionally, and financially following the shock of my mother's death and the aftermath. I was not ready to go back to work. I needed money for groceries, but there was nothing in my pocketbook. I decided to walk to the bank to double-check my balance at the ATM. It was on Saturday and the bank was closed. At the time, technology had not advanced to the point where I could use any communication device to see if I had enough money to buy a few items at the grocery store. When I arrived at the ATM and pulled out my card, I was stunned to find ten twenty-dollar bills sitting in the withdrawal tray. I panicked. The bank was closed, there were no cars in the parking lot, and there was no one around. I did not know what to do. Should I leave the money alone and walk away or should I take it?

I decided to take the money and return it to the bank on the next business day. And that was what I did. To my surprise, an employee told me to have a seat while the bank audited the ATM to make sure that all transactions were performed accurately. I patiently waited. After a while the bank confirmed that there were no discrepancies or shortages involving withdrawals and deposits at the ATM. Furthermore, no one had performed any transaction in that dollar amount on the machine that day and no one had called the bank about missing money, so the money was given back to me. I could not believe how the Lord knew to provide for my needs and how he could show mercy on a sinner like me. Forevermore, I will thank him for his miraculous providences in my life.

Jesus, My Strength and My Redeemer

After those dark days, I clung to the cross of Jesus Christ more than ever. I found joy only in reading the Scriptures and hearing his Word. I worshipped three days out of the week and served others. That was the only thing that kept me from thinking about my past predicaments. Jesus Christ had a plan for my life, so he watched over me day and night. He nourished, comforted, and strengthened me from year to year. I felt better through the help of the resurrection power of the Holy Spirit. Whenever I do his will, I am trying to know him better. May Jesus help us all accomplish our goals in him to inherit life everlasting.

Jesus, My Deliverer

L ate one Friday afternoon I backed my car out of the garage to go to church for a worship service. Our house was on a hill that sloped down to the street. I started the engine but mistakenly put the car in neutral instead of reverse. When the car slid backward, I tried to shift into park, but it was too late. The car was now in motion. I opened the driver-side door and stuck one foot out. Why I did that I do not know, but my one foot was in the car while the other was on the ground. The car's motion pressed my foot to the ground and twisted my body against my neighbor's fence. I was caught between the fence and the car. I tried to step on the brakes, but nothing happened because the car was in neutral and threatening to head down the hill.

I was being crushed against the fence by my car. My next-door neighbor tried to help by pushing the car to the front of the garage, but she was unable to do this. The car was heavier than she thought. The car remained at the middle of the hill. She quickly ran into her house and brought back a hammer to break down the fence, but as soon as she started to do this, the car began to go backward again, pushing me against the fence and toward the ground. The car would run over me as soon as the fence went down. My neighbor stopped attacking the fence and desperately held on to it against the car. Meanwhile, I screamed for help. At that time of day, most of the people in the neighborhood were stay-at-home moms whose husbands were at work. At that point in my ordeal, there was no guarantee about what would happen next. My children joined the effort to push the car upward to stop it from running over me.

When I think of the miracles of God, mysteries of his creation, his attributes and redemptive purposes for humanity, salvation through his only Son Christ Jesus, his grace and life everlasting; I always want to shout Hallelujah to glorify his Holy Name until end of my days. Humanity does not know how much the Father loves them; he always thinks good thoughts about his children, whether we pay much attentions to him or not; he still yearns to have relationship with his own creation every day; therefore, let us draw more closer to him in fellowships, to have eternal relationships with him; the Father loves our worshipping him in the beauty of his holiness. Praise his Holy Name! Amen and Amen!

God's ways are mysterious. As I continued to scream, out of nowhere from the back of a house directly across the street appeared a slender man about five foot six, wearing reading glasses and walking a little dog. There was no pathway leading from the back of that house to the front, and there was a fence around the house behind it. We lived in a neighborhood where everybody knew everybody. No one knew this guy or had seen him before. However, he came running to my rescue.

The man used his shoulders to push the car forward to the front of the garage. I fell to the ground. The muscles in my left foot were crushed, but I had no broken bone. The accident had put a deep dent in my flesh, and the bruises and smashed-up veins left scars on my legs that remain today. My deliverer stepped on the brakes, put the car in park, walked over, and picked me up from the ground. All this time, he spoke to no one. He walked through my kitchen, carrying me on his shoulders into the living room, and laid me down on the couch. The only words he spoke were to my daughter. "Now you can call the ambulance to take her to the hospital," he said. Then he quickly walked out.

Though I was in great pain, I asked for his name and phone number so I could get in touch and offer him my appreciation for saving my life, but to my surprise he had disappeared. I asked my children and neighborhood kids to run after him in different directions and get a hold of him, but he was gone, nowhere to be found. *What just happened?* I asked myself. Our house was located on a dead-end street. The neighborhood kids searched all over for this slender man with the little dog, but no one found him. Everyone saw him when he was performing his rescue mission, but now he had vanished. I saw him run to rescue me and observed where he came from, but when he left no one saw which direction he took. He was gone forever.

Everyone wondered what had happened and everyone was focused on finding him and learning who he was and where he had come from. But no one was able to locate him anywhere in the neighborhood. And as slender as he was, how was he able to push my car up the hill to the front of the garage without anyone's help? How come he didn't ask what had happened to me, give me his name, or come back to check on me? Where did he come from and how did he disappear? I still have not found answers to these questions. We never heard from this man again, and only Jesus Christ knows the solution to this mystery.

I Sought the LORD in Distress

In the wilderness, I cry unto the Father; "Oh my Father, my Father LORD, where are you? Hear my voice, give ear to my prayers and supplications, have mercy on me, O my Father LORD; the true, righteous Father, my soul dwells in darkness of the deep, where there is no way out; my enemies rise against me day and night; I need your help; you are the only Father that can prevail against my enemies and deliver me out of my distress; when I remember how merciful you are, your love for me, your faithfulness through the years; I just want to say Thank you, I Trust you; may your will be done in Jesus Name!"

Amen and amen!

Be Still and Know
That I Am God!

One evening, a news report said there would be a tornado watch for the area throughout the night. The children panicked. I assured them that Jesus would not allow anything to happen to us, because we believe in him. Sure enough, the tornado warning siren went off in the middle of the night. We ran down to the basement and took shelter. When the tornado hit the neighborhood, it sounded like the world had spun around and was coming to an end. It was a horrific experience. We heard trees falling and a clattering upstairs, but we did not leave the basement until the noise finally ceased, the wind died down, and the siren stopped sounding. We waited until we felt we would be safe.

It was still dark, so we thanked God for saving our lives and went to bed, not knowing what damage had occurred in the neighborhood. To our surprise, we discovered in the morning that Jesus had done wonders again. The tornado had left the neighborhood in terrible disarray, with uprooted trees and shredded roofs. The houses behind, beside, and in front of ours all suffered damage, but our house was untouched. People in the neighborhood were amazed that every home was damaged except ours. Even a giant pear tree in our backyard was spared, though the tornado uprooted trees in almost everyone else's yard.

This was not magic. It was the Lord's doing, and it was marvelous in our eyes. The Father's love for us was made manifest.

I glorify you, O my Father!

I will Praise thee, Oh LORD my Father;

I will Praise and give you all the Glory;

For there is no other God like unto thee;

The Earth and Heavens declare your Glory;

The Moon, Stars, Oceans, Rivers and Seas;

The Forest, Desert, Mountains, Hills and Valleys;

Are all your handiworks

You make ways through desert lands, Oceans, Rivers;

Where there seems to be no pathways;

You heal diseases; without physicians diagnosis or remedies;

I Praise your Holy Name forever and ever more.

Amen!

(Ivy Oppan-2015)

Jehovah-Nissi: the Lord, Our Banner

One evening when I arrived home from work, I found a newly installed fire hydrant in front of our house by the mailbox. I did not like having it there. "With all the houses on the street," I asked, "why did the village decide to install this fire hydrant in front of ours? Why not any other house in the neighborhood?" I was not happy. Anytime I looked out of our front window, the hydrant was the first thing I saw. The sight kept me from admiring our two small crab apple trees. "You do not have a choice," my husband said. "The hydrant is on the sidewalk, and that belongs to the village."

I grumbled about the hydrant for months. Then one evening, the children and I were eating dinner and discussing the day when someone smelled smoke. I quickly got up from the dining room table and checked the kitchen to see what was burning, but nothing was broiling or baking in the oven. I sat back down and we continued eating and talking, after another minute, I smelled the smoke. When I turned around to look into the living room on the other side of the kitchen, I saw fire leaping up from my bedroom. It had already engulfed all of the bedrooms and was on its way to the living room and the kitchen.

In my bedroom was a television set with an extension cord running to an outlet on the bathroom wall. The cord had been on the bedroom carpet for years and seemed to be fine. Little did I realize that by walking over the cord all those years we had caused the rubber shield to wear out, the exposed wiring had touched the carpet and set the house on fire; I ran toward the bedroom to try to do something about the situation, but it was too late, smoke and fire filled the house; the children ran outside. They screamed at me to leave, but I was determined to save my treasures. I am glad that they called me out of the burning house, because I could have died from the smoke. The house was dark and the fire was raging. I had to leave earthly things behind or perish.

I believe a neighbor called the fire department. As it turned out, the only fire hydrant on the street was sitting in front of my house. This was not mere chance. Jesus Christ knew what the Enemy planned to do to us and installed the fire hydrant to thwart that scheme. We ought to give glory to the Lord in all situations, good and bad. Jesus knows everything and will take control no matter what our troubles may be. The Enemy meant us harm, but Jesus has a plan to work out everything for the good for the glory of his holy name.

Our small town had a volunteer fire department. Firefighters had to be contacted at their houses to report to the scene of a blaze. We waited in the yard for twenty-five minutes, watching all of our earthly possessions burn to ashes. There was nothing anyone could do but wait. When the firefighters finally arrived, they hooked up their hoses to the hydrant that I had complained about and quenched the fire. I was thankful to our Lord for being so thoughtful to our family and for doing such a mighty act. He is worthy of praise forevermore.

When the fire was finally out, there was nothing left except ashes and our detached garage. However, we were all alive with no burns on our bodies, and we lived to tell of the Lord's goodness and mercies, which never fail. They are renewed every morning. We are grateful to the Lord forevermore.

My Prayer to the LORD for Deliverance

"I sought the LORD, the LORD heard me. Then the Heavens broke up my behalf with illuminating lights; there appeared showers of blessings from above, I heard sounds of thunderstorms coming into the pit to resurrect my soul out of darkness of the deep; into the illuminating lights of the Almighty God; I am delivered; Praise the LORD, delivered by his Word, once I was in bondage of the enemy; but now delivered by the death and resurrection of Christ my Lord and Savior; I glorify Jesus for redeeming my soul out of darkness into his Marvelous lights forever.!

Amen and amen!

A Covenant-Keeping God

W hen our Lord wants things done on earth, he chooses his instruments for those purposes from among humanity. If those who answer the call persevere through all trials, his purposes will be revealed in them.

"Furthermore, whosoever the Father fore ordains, them he also called; when they are called, then he proves them righteous, when proven righteous, he magnifies them; therefore, if the Father does all these things in his Sovereignty; who is able to question his ways?"

After responding to the call, I enjoyed being in the house of the Lord and serving him in any capacity. The journey was not easy, and I overcame several battles only by his grace. It took me several years to give up my secular job and fully serve the Lord. I worked full time, raised four children, and still tried to function in his will.

However, I could sense that something was wrong. When I made money, it seemed as if I was bringing home ice cubes that melted away before I could account for them. The Enemy took me for a ride while I desired to own every new thing on the market. Though I might not need an item, I had to buy it. I worked harder and studied harder but got nowhere. I filled in for others on my days off and skipped lunch and break periods to make sure that work went smoothly, but nothing was happening for me. Jesus was telling me, "My child, you do not belong in the secular world. You belong to me. Give up your job and come to me, and I will give you rest." Leaving my job to follow him was difficult. I am still trying to understand myself, and I periodically ask myself, *"was I dreaming when I made the decision to surrender everything for the gospel's sake?"*

I had talked to Jesus several times over the years about quitting my job but was not able to yield to the Holy Spirit's will. Three months before I finally did my daughter Daisy and I went to a midweek service. The pastor preached about obeying the call of God to serve humanity. I was not a regular worshipper in this congregation, and I realized that the pastor knew nothing about me. I felt that it was time for me to surrender to the Lord. After the service, Daisy looked me in the eye and said, "It seemed that the preacher was talking to you. Are you going to do it?" I smiled and said, "I will do it!"

However, I wondered how I would survive without an income. I did not quit working, but darkness overwhelmed my soul. No matter how hard I tried to fall asleep, I would be up until daybreak. For three months, I could barely get four hours of sleep each night. I lived in fear and anxiety. I was miserable. I felt pressure, but I could not tell exactly what was wrong. I was upset and restless, and I thought about the issue day and night, not knowing what to do.

One afternoon at work, I received a phone call from a man of God. He said that the Lord had asked him to tell me to give up my job and to follow after his will. He said that my grace period to work was over. He asked me to give him a call when I got home from work that evening. I did, and after he shared the rest of the Lord's message, I knew it was time to quit my job and surrender to God's will. I had no choice but to obey him and to leave the consequences in his hands.

The following morning, I decided to end the ordeal and yield to Jesus. When I arrived at work, the first thing I did was to write my resignation letter. As soon as the manager came through the door, I followed her to her office and gave her the letter. "What is this?" she asked. "My resignation letter," I replied. She asked me to put it in her tray. I did that and left her office. At the end of two weeks, she talked with me about my decision. I could not explain why I needed to leave but said, "It is done." She accepted my decision and I finally left my job that day. To my surprise, as soon as I left for home, peace overwhelmed my soul, the dark cloud hanging over my head for three months lifted, and I entered a realm of joy. I believe that heaven was happy that I had the courage to do what was right in the eyes of the Lord of Hosts.

My husband Anthony normally picked me up at the train station. That evening when we met, I said, "Guess what: it is done."

"What is done?" he asked.

I said I finally had the courage to quit my job.

"You did?" he said. Anthony was doubtful because for two years I had talked about quitting every week but it had never happened. When I had told him of my decision two weeks before that evening, he thought I was just talking again.

"What will you eat?" he asked.

"If I have nothing to eat, I will cry to the Lord," I said.

Anthony was quiet for a moment and then said, "Are you kidding me?"

"No, I am not kidding you," I told him. "Today was my last day at work, and I am not going back. It is done."

I did not know what my next step in faith would be, but I trusted Jesus to direct my path in his righteousness. That night I slept like I had not slept in years. I had a good eight hours of sleep with no worries or fears. I was freed from the Enemy's bondage and entered a new era to serve Jesus Christ.

I was already doing the Lord's work on all three service days at my church, so I asked for guidance to continue to do his will. I resumed my position as a worker at the same church where I had once served Jesus for several years. Now I had time to attend all services, something I could not do before when I was busy. I worked as an assistant to the pastor. Everything seemed to be fine for about a year. When believers make up their minds to follow the Lord and to serve him, the Enemy will do everything in his power to stop God's glory from shining through their lives.

Birthing of
El-Elohim Ministries

W hen I realized that my calling was to serve in that church, I persevered. No matter what was happening in my family or what the weather conditions, I remained faithful to the call. I overcame every hindrance by the blood of Jesus Christ. However, the Lord allows his chosen ones to face adversity for his glory. A few months before the birthing of El-Elohim Ministries, Daily Internet Ministry, ordained by Jesus Christ to spread the gospel of his second coming all over the face of the earth. I faced a great trial in the church. The Lord commissioned me for a much higher position. He instructed me in a dream to start ministering in all churches. I was to serve him everywhere possible, in all branches of the church. It was time for me to move forward. I had served him in one place for twenty years with no progress in my calling.

As soon as I revealed what was told to me in the dream to an elder in the church, enemy forces instigated plans to persecute me out of the congregation. I was in the Lord's will and was a dedicated worker, but suddenly I became a problem for the church that I had served for twenty long years. Enemies rose up against me every worship day. Curses and condemnations were my thanks for years of dedication to the church. My enemies fought me on everything from my status in the church to the chair that I sat on every Sunday to a bottle of drinking water.

Though I had assisted the pastor as an oracle of God for several years, suddenly I could no longer advise him on any issue. When he made his own decisions concerning the church, members fought him because they thought these were my ideas. The persecution grew stronger every worship day. Insults and disgraceful words rained down on me from the pulpit through the congregation. Everybody had a problem with me, though I did nothing to anyone. Words cannot express what I endured physically, emotionally, and spiritually. I faced nights of affliction and years of agony. However, the stronger the battle against me, the more the hand of the Lord protected me from my enemies. I decided to fast and to pray and to seek the Lord's mercy and deliverance.

As I suffered, Jesus was working to deliver me. Sooner than I thought, he set me free from the bondage of enemy forces. I sought the Lord to know what he had for me to do on days when I did not serve him at church. He enlightened me about what to do next. I set up an Internet ministry to preach the good news throughout the world. When I started, I thought I was just filling in off-days, but I was not. The Lord revealed that my assignment was to preach the gospel of the second coming to all nations. For this, I was called out of darkness into the light. As soon as my ministry started, the Lord asked me to preach the gospel full time. However, the Enemy was not happy and started to plague me in the church. The Lord asked me to leave my comfort zone and to serve him in other churches. Therefore I started moving from one branch to another every Sunday to avoid persecution from my church. I became happier because although I was not in my post every Sunday, I was still in the will of the Father and without the curses and persecutions that I endured on service days.

At first, my adversaries took delight in having cast me out of the church. However, when they realized that I was much happier than when I had been in their midst, they gathered together and sought to return me to my former position on Sundays so they could control my movements as before. No matter what I did, it was not acceptable to them. The Adversary was at work and wanted to steal my joy at all costs. But my opponents could not stop the glory of God from shining throughout the churches. In all my trials, the Lord was faithful to me and protected my life from all fiery darts and dangers from enemy forces. I give glory, honor, and adoration to Him forevermore.

"I AM THAT I AM!"
Says the Lord of Hosts

One Sunday morning in April 2013, the Lord spoke to a seer in a vision and sent her to me with a message that changed my life forever. She told me, "Thus said the Lord of Hosts: tell my beloved that before September 2013, I will do something unique in her life that shall make all ears tingle."

"What is it that the Lord wants to do, and what shall I do to qualify for it?" I asked.

"I do not know," she replied. "Just continue to praise, to worship, and to offer thanks to him."

After few weeks a prophetess from a different branch of the church gave me a word from the Lord to fast from meat for three months for his glory. This was not easy, but I delight in obeying the Lord, so I fasted. Toward the end of the three months, I received several manifestations of the Holy Spirit in dreams and visions. In one dream, I found myself in the presence of the Lord of Hosts. He anointed me, and clothed me with a garment of lights that shone like the sun, saying, "This will be your garment of glory henceforth." The garment resembled the robe of a bishop or a senior evangelist with purple lace trimming on the cape and with three purple crosses and purple frills. I was amazed at what the Lord of Hosts had done.

"Lord, this garment has never been worn by any woman in the church," I said.

"I ordain and commission you with this garment," he replied. "Go and wear it for my glory."

I glorified his holy name in the dream but woke up not knowing what to do. *What did I do to find this kind of favor in the eyes of the Lord of Hosts?* I wondered. In fact, I had done nothing, nor had I prayed for this to happen to me. It was only by his grace that he counted me worthy to be in his presence for anointment, ordination, and commissioning to manifest his glory. He would use me for purposes known to him and to Jesus Christ. Many took this as my own doing, but what would I have been trying to prove? As far as I was concerned, I was simply following the Lord's instructions.

"Thus said the LORD unto me, I will do something new, all ears shall tingle, and you will give me Praises forever. Look, what the LORD has done! He gave me his words and fulfilled his words! He did that which he said he will do; the LORD is merciful, gracious and faithful in all his ways! Who can do all things? Help me to Praise the LORD, for his Mercies endures forever. He is about to do it for you as well; believe in the Father with your minds, soul and body; for then the LORD will command his blessings even life for evermore."

Amen and amen!

After the ordination, I received instructions to prepare for the next phase of my calling. After many years, I still was not aware of why the Lord had called me. All I knew was that my heart was yearning to do his will. I obeyed him and made the garment as instructed. However, because no woman in the church anywhere in the world had ever worn such a garment, this became a big problem. Opponents rose up against me.

An angel of the Lord appeared to me in a dream and warned me that Satan was after the regalia and that I should not allow him to take it away from me. "You were ordained and commissioned and given a garment by the Lord of Hosts," the angel said. "Do not disobey him by failing to do what he asked you to do." When I awoke, I said, "Oh yeah!" Then I made the robe. I did not know when or how the Lord of Hosts wanted things done with the regalia, so I kept it at the church for a year, awaiting the Lord's instructions.

A year later, an angel of the Lord appeared to me in a dream, questioning why I had made certain decisions in the previous year and asking what was important to me about my assignment. I was not aware that I was being tested, but I answered all the questions to the best of my knowledge. The angel congratulated me and gave me titles. "These titles accompany the regalia given to you by the Lord of Hosts," the angel said. "You passed the test." Then he disappeared from the vision. I knew then that the Lord had judged me to be worthy to wear the garment for his glory. That was why he gave me the titles to go along with the regalia. After this vision, I continued to offer special prayers, asking for the Lord's directions about what to do next. Angels in similar robes continually instructed me in my dreams to bring me up to the standards of the regalia.

One Sunday after services, a prophetess gave me a word from the Lord, telling me the date and the place to wear the garment for his glory. The Lord had said he would do something that made all ears tingle. He was faithful to his word. All ears did tingle and still do! However, an angel of the Lord had revealed to me in a dream that the Adversary would try to stop me from carrying out the will of the Father. I fasted and prayed, asking the Lord to help me do what he had ordained, and he strengthened me through the Holy Spirit.

On that fateful morning, I was empowered from on high to manifest his glory for the world to see. However, when members of the church saw the garment I wore, persecutions arose against me on a higher level. Men and women of God who had known me for years turned against me, slandered me, spread rumors, and rained curses on me. No woman in the history of the church had ever sown or worn that kind of a garment. However, the Lord was with me throughout the ordeal. I was asked to keep the garment away from the church, but I was not about to undo what the Lord had done. I did not care about pleasing humanity. Therefore I took a break from the church and kept the garment, awaiting directions from the Lord.

A week earlier, a messenger of the Lord had warned me in a dream not to make any more white garments. A day before, I had purchased white fabric to do just that. The angel directed me to give the fabric as a gift to a certain person. When I awoke from the dream that morning, I took the fabric to the church, told my pastor about the angel's warning, and gave away the fabric to the person the angel had identified.

The angel had told me to take a break from the church. At that point, I did not understand that the Lord wanted me to kick off my new ministry and to concentrate on spreading the gospel to the world. However, when I took off, I was able to focus and received wisdom, knowledge, and understanding from the Holy Spirit to move the ministry forward. When I took a break from the church, I thought that I just needed to clear my mind of the problems I had faced. I did not know that my steps were already ordered from above and that this was the appropriate time to focus on the assignment for which I had been chosen by Jesus Christ.

Beware of the Adversary

As a church worker, I participated in Friday prayers, which started at midnight and ended about 2:00 a.m. Because of the distance between the church and my house, I would normally rest and stay until daybreak before leaving for home. However, one Friday, I decided to leave for home immediately after the service was over. No one could understand why I would want to drive home in the early morning hours when I had not gotten any sleep, but I was determined to leave and no one could stop me. The trip was difficult, for I was exhausted and ready to sleep, but I reached my driveway and parked the car. Little did I know that I was about to face the ugliest warfare that the Enemy had ever planned for me.

I picked up my hand luggage and stepped out of the car. As I walked across the driveway, I suddenly saw an enormous black bird sitting at my front door, waiting to attack me. I did not know that coming home that morning would be the biggest mistake I had ever made. Only the Lord knows why he allowed me to leave the church to face the Enemy's attack. The huge bird slapped my face with its wings. The blows were strong enough to push me backward and to knock the luggage out of my hand. I screamed as the huge bird flew over my head, crowing jubilantly. I stood frozen, looking up at the bird. I was stunned. This was the most terrifying experience of my life. I watched the evil bird disappear into the skies, still celebrating its victory over me.

I picked up my luggage and opened the front door. I dropped the luggage at the threshold and wondered what might happen to me next. *Will I survive this attack, or am I about to drop dead?* I asked myself. Suddenly the Holy Spirit spoke to me, saying, "Be strong in my resurrection power. Take a cup of water and wash your face. Kneel down, sing a song of victory, and thank the Lord for saving your life."

I followed the Holy Spirit's instructions, but I could not sleep for fear of the unknown. Would I die, or would I go blind? I was not sure how many hours it might take for evil to manifest itself. I grabbed my Bible and started to read, but I could not concentrate. I kept on thinking, *What if I had not come back home at that hour? Would the evil bird still have been waiting at my front door? And why did the Enemy plan this attack on my life?*

Morning finally arrived, but I was still shaken from the attack. I told my husband what had happened, but I do not think he understood. He looked at me as if I were telling a make-believe story.

I fasted and prayed for the Lord to sustain my life. Night after night I read my Bible and prayed until the seventh day when I felt a little sick. However, the Lord had saved me from the hands of the Enemy, and I had lived to tell the world that God is good to all who trust and believe in him.

Thank you, Jesus Christ, for saving my soul from the Enemy. I appreciate your grace given to me freely forevermore. Amen!

Conclusion

I would like to thank you for taking the time to read about these revelations and manifestations of Jesus Christ. I hope these testimonies have inspired you to believe in the Prince of Peace, who suffered for our iniquities, died on the cross of Calvary, went to Hades to set the captives free, and rose again from the dead to redeem all humanity from bondage into salvation, grace, and life everlasting.

Though I relate to humanity these revelations and manifestations, I claim no glory but give it all to the Lord of Hosts. This book contains what Jesus Christ has given to me by grace, and nothing stems my own human imagination.

Our Lord and Savior Jesus Christ is calling workers for his vineyard every day. If you should hear his voice, do not hinder him but follow after his will and be a useful servant for his glory forevermore.

Amen and amen!

Vote of Thanks to JEHOVAH

"Blessed be the Name of Jehovah! Blessed be the Name of the Almighty in the Beauty of his Holiness; Blessed be his Holy Name in his Sovereignty; Blessed be his Holy Name for his Miraculous works; Blessed be his Holy Name based on his Supremacy; Blessed be his Holy Name with sounds of adoration and dance; Blessed be his

Holy Name with instruments of guitars and organs; Blessed be his Holy Name upon the loud cymbals; Blessed be his Holy Name upon high sounding cymbals. Let all creation of the Almighty God bless him; blessed be his Holy Name! Bless the Holy Name of JEHOVAH forever."

Amen and amen!

A Quote from Christ to Humanity

"I Jesus commissioned my messenger to attest to humanity, these revelations in tabernacles. I am the root, the seed of David, the shinning, morning star. I am the Holy Spirit, the bride, saying; Come quickly! Let him that is thirsty come unto me, and whosoever will let him come unto me and drink from the wells of Living waters freely forever.

Amen and amen!

Printed in the United States
By Bookmasters